"I believe Christians must become involved in politics as elected officials, candidates, and campaign workers, to strengthen and preserve our great nation by ensuring that it remains "One nation under God." Christians have stayed aloof from politics for too long. When prayers are banned from schools, preachers of the gospel are denied freedom of speech, and our moral standards have reached the lowest levels, surely it is time for Christians to act!"

Leo Berman, City Councilman, Arlington, Texas

Leo Berman is currently a State Representative for the State of Texas, 6th District 2012.

TURNING POINTS

how DECEPTION steals freedoms

TERRY W. BETTIS

ARPress
ILLUMINATING IDEAS
EMPOWERING VOICES

ARPress
45 Dan Road Suite 5
Canton MA 02021

Hotline: 1(888) 821-0229
Fax: 1(508) 545-7580

Ordering Information:
Quantity sales. Special discounts are available on quantity purchases by corporations, associations, and others. For details, contact the publisher at the address above.

Printed in the United States of America.

ISBN-13: Paperback   979-8-89389-563-6
          eBook   979-8-89389-564-3

Library of Congress Control Number: 2024920612

The Eve of Rebellion
The First Turning Point

"We cannot be happy without being free; we cannot be free without being secure in our property; we cannot be secure in our property if, without our consent, others may, as by right, take it away; taxes imposed on us by Parliament do thus take it away."

– John Dickinson, 1776

Taxation was the tempest that would eventually lead the people to rebel against the Crown (The Stamp Act).

Will taxation upon the people be the Turning Point for a second rebellion by the *taxed*?

DEDICATION TO:

All the PATRIOTS that believe in this COUNTRY

My Wife: Billie K. Bettis

My daughters & their spouses,

Marla Joyner (Bettis) & Husband Dusty Joyner

Micah R. (Bettis) Heady & Husband Gary Heady

Erin E. (Bettis) Delozier & Husband Cody Delozier

My Grandchildren,

Kaitlyn, Chase, Wade, Cole, Brooklyn, Levi, Seth, Bailey

Bradley & Kaley

SPECIAL THANKS TO

Leo Berman
Jeanie Coates
Timothy Lamb
Marla Joyner
Linda Montoya
Thomas G. West
William A. Schambra
Gail Odegaard
(For her brilliant thoughts on the Cover graphics of this book)

FORWARD

Christianity addresses itself to every aspect of life – the home, school, community, business and politics – as well as to the church. It involves everything we do and is a way of thinking, speaking, and behaving.

Our Christian belief requires that we become involved in government and bear witness to the truth that our nation became great because of our faith in God. The very foundation of our nation was built upon Christian principles as we launch ourselves as:

"One Nation under God"

Today many are working to deny our Christian origins, to defy God and thus, however unwittingly, to destroy our nation. To remain a great nation, we must have Christian leadership at every level of government. Paul wrote:[1] "To aspire to leadership is an honorable ambition." He described Christian leaders as above reproach faithful to their wives, sober, temperate, courteous, hospitable and good teachers, not given to drink or brawling, or a forbearing disposition, avoiding quarrels, and not lovers of money. No one can meet those standards through mere human wisdom and power. Only Jesus was perfect and pure. But we Christians must involve ourselves politically to seek out individuals who approach Paul's description of a Christian leader and are willing to live and lead by faith in Christ, then work hard to elect them to office.

Unfortunately, there are too few Christian leaders in government today. As a result, we are experiencing a devastating erosion of moral standards in our nation. This deterioration is typified by an absence of ethics in government, a glorification of sex and violence, an increase in drug

---

1   1 Timothy 3:1

and alcohol use, accompanied by rising crime rates, and a proliferation of socialism. The latter has progressed to the point that millions of individuals are relinquishing responsibility, initiative, and self-respect to the government and relying on government rather than on God.

My personal philosophy is based on a deep belief in God and in exercising common sense in government.

It is best described in the words of President Lincoln, who in 1859 wrote the following in a letter to his brother: "You cannot bring about prosperity, by discouraging thrift. You cannot strengthen the weak, by weakening the strong.

"You cannot bring about prosperity, by discouraging thrift. You cannot strengthen the weak, by weakening the strong.
You cannot help the wage earner, by pulling down the wage payer.

You cannot further the brotherhood of man, by encouraging class hatred. You cannot help the poor, by destroying the rich. You cannot establish sound security, on borrowed money.

You cannot keep out of trouble, by spending more than you earn.

You cannot build character and courage, by taking away man's initiative and independence.

You cannot help man permanently, by doing for them what they would and should do for themselves."

President Lincoln wrote the letter to his brother, and I applaud him, however, he probably never thought the progressives would infiltrate the government and pass laws and mandates upon the people. And, through those laws would slowly start the destruction of the Constitution of America and the Bill of Rights.

Alexander Hamilton said,
"A nation which can prefer disgrace to danger is prepared for a master and deserves one."

TABLE OF CONTENTS

Chapter 1

The Eve of Rebellion – 1773

Turning Points

In 1773, Philadelphia threatens Tea Men. Parliament, faced with rebellion and crippling commercial boycott, repealed the Stamp Act in 1766. The next year the Ministry devised a light indirect tax on TEA which, being external, presumably met the colonial objections to a direct tax. Opposition to the new levy was fading when in 1773; the London officials granted a monopoly of the tea business in America to the powerful and the hated British East India Company. These arrangements would make the tea, even with the three-penny tax included, cheaper than ever. The colonials, resenting this *transparent* attempt to trick them into paying the tax, staged several famous tea parties. Those in Boston and at New York involved throwing the tea overboard; the affair at Annapolis resulted in the burning of both vessels and the cargo. At Portsmouth and Philadelphia, the tea ships were turned away. Of the reasons here given by the Philadelphians for action, determined which was the strongest, and whether it was strong enough to warrant the measures threatened.

Patrick Henry Demanded Boldness (1775)

[2]Daniel Leonard's well-justified lack of confidence in the ill-trained colonial militia was more than shared by the Earl of Sandwich. In the House of the Lords he scorned the colonials as "raw, undisciplined, cowardly men," and hoped that they would assemble 200,000 "brave fellows" rather than 50,000.

2   The American Spirit, Vol. 1, pg 97

"They tell us, sir that we are weak; unable to cope with so formidable an adversary. But when shall we be stronger? Will it be next week, or the next year? Will it be when we are totally disarmed, and when a British guard shall be stationed in every house? Shall we gather strength by irresolution and inaction? Shall we acquire the means of effectual resistance by lying supinely on our backs and hugging the delusive phantom of hope, until our enemies shall have bound us hand and foot?"...

There is much more to this story that would lead up to the Declaration and the battle for Independence and Liberty for America.

There are two conflicting versions to the Clash of Arms in the Battle for Independence.

AMERICAN VERSION

At Lexington... a company of militia... mustered near the meeting house. The (British) troops came in sight of them just before sunrise; and running within a few rods of them, the Commanding Officer (Pitcairn) accosted the militia in words to this effect: "Disperse, you rebels-damn you, throw down your arms and disperse"; upon which the troops huzzaed, and immediately one or two officers discharged their pistols, which were instantaneously followed by the firing of four or five of the soldiers, and then there seemed to a general discharge from the whole body. Eight of our men were killed and nine wounded....

In Lexington (the British) . . . also set fire to several other houses. They pillaged almost every house they passed. But the savage barbarity exercised

upon the bodies of our unfortunate brethren who fell is almost incredible. Not contented with shooting down the unarmed, aged, and infirm, they disregarded the cries of the wounded, killing them without mercy, and mangling their bodies in the most shocking manner.

BRITISH VERSION

. . . Six companies of (British) light infantry at Lexington found a body of the country people under arms, on a green close to the road. And upon the King's troops marching up to them, in order to inquire the reason of their being so assembled, they went off in great confusion. And several guns were fired upon the King's troops from behind a stone wall, and also from the meeting-house and other houses, by which one man was wounded, and Major Pitcairn's horse was shot in two places. In consequence of this attack by the rebels, the troops returned the fire and killed several of them . . .

On the return of the troops from Concord, they (the rebels) . . . began to fire upon them from behind stone walls and houses and kept up in that manner a scattering fire during the whole of their march of fifteen miles, by which means several were killed and wounded. And such was the cruelty and barbarity of the rebels that they scalped and cut off the ears of some of the wounded men who fell into their hands.

Franklin wrote a letter to Mr. Strahan, after the news at Lexington and Concord:

[3]"You are a member of Parliament, and one of those majorities which has doomed my country to destruction. You have begun to burn our towns and murder our people. Look upon your hands! They are stained with the blood of your relations! You and I were long friends; you are now my enemy, and I am yours." B. Franklin

"One has to know history to understand current events." Terry W. Bettis 7/1/2010

"The battle started over taxes and more government control. My friends, where are we today." 7/1/2010

---

3   To William Strahan, July 5, 1776, in A. E. Smyth, ed., The Writings of Benjamin Franklin (1906), VI, 407

Chapter 2

State Nullification Expanding Their Powers

Turning Points

No sooner had the Constitution and Amendments been ratified, and the federalists began working to expand their powers. The Alien and Sedition Act (the original version of the Patriot Act and Homeland Security???) punished speech, even though this was a power specifically reserved to the States. The Kentucky Resolutions show that nullification of usurpations, non-delegated powers was the proper remedy for the States and People to take. Very interesting and important reading, especially today as the States are now "pushing back" against the federal power. Please take time to read this important historical document. Bottom line: we are in full legal right to ignore and nullify offending federal law and decisions, but it will take courage and sacrifice to take back what is ours. Heaven helps us in our resolution to conform all human institutions to the gospel, especially our government.

These laws raised the residency requirements for citizenship from 5 to 14 years, authorized the President to deport aliens, and permitted their arrest, imprisonment, and deportation during wartime. The Sedition Act made it a crime for American citizens to "print, utter, or publish . . . any false, scandalous, and malicious writing" about the Government.

The laws were directed against Democratic-Republicans, the party typically favored by new citizens, and the only journalists prosecuted under the Sedition Act were editors of Democratic-Republican newspapers. Sedition Act trials, along with the Senate's use of its contempt powers to suppress dissent, set off a firestorm of criticism against the Federalists and contributed to their defeat in the election of 1800, after which the acts were repealed or allowed to expire. The controversies surrounding them, however, provided for some of the first testing's of the limits of freedom of speech and press.

For more information, visit The National Archives' Treasures of Congress Online Exhibit.

Acts, Bills, and Laws, 1798

In 1798, the Federalist-controlled Congress passed a series of laws which, on the surface, were designed to control the activities of foreigners in the United States during a time of impending war. Beneath the surface, however, the real intent of these laws was to destroy Jeffersonian Republicanism. The laws, known collectively as the "Alien and Sedition Acts," included:

- The Naturalization Act, which extended the residency period from 5 to 14 years for those aliens seeking citizenship; this law was aimed at Irish and French immigrants who were often active in Republican politics

- The Alien Act, which allowed the expulsion of aliens deemed dangerous during peacetime

- The Alien Enemies Act, which allowed the expulsion or imprisonment of aliens deemed dangerous during wartime. This was never enforced, but it did prompt numerous Frenchmen to return home

- The Sedition Act, which provided for fines or imprisonment for individuals who criticized the government, Congress, or president in speech or print

Sedition campaign poster, 1800

The Alien Acts were never enforced, but the Sedition Act was. A number of Republican newspaper publishers were convicted under the terms of this law. The Jeffersonian argued quite rightly that the Sedition Act violated the terms of the First Amendment and offered a remedy in the Virginia and Kentucky Resolutions.

While these laws were either repealed or allowed to expire in the next administration, they were significant as rallying points for the Jeffersonian. The heavy-handed Federalist policies worked to the advantage of the Republicans as they prepared for the Election of 1800.

http://www.historycentral.com/documents/AlienSedition.html

Alien and Sedition Acts: Order versus Liberty

When Congress passed the Alien and Sedition Acts in 1798; it opened a heated debate about the limits of freedom in a free society. By Larry Gragg on July 4, 1798…

http://www.historynet.com/ah/blorderverusliberty

The Kentucky Resolutions of 1798
By Thomas Jefferson

The Kentucky Resolutions of 1798 were written secretly by Thomas Jefferson in response to *the Alien and Sedition Acts* passed by the federal government. The laws were judged to be unconstitutional by Virginia and Kentucky

1. *Resolved,* That the several States composing, the United States of America, are not united on the principle of unlimited submission to their general government; but that, by a compact under the style and title of a Constitution for the United States, and of amendments thereto, they constituted a general government for special purposes delegated to that government certain definite powers, reserving, each State to itself, the residuary mass of right to their own self-government; and that when-so-ever the general government assumes un-delegated powers, its acts are un-authoritative, void, and of no force: that to this compact each State acceded as a State, and is an integral part, its co-States forming, as to itself, the other party: that the government created by this compact was not made the exclusive or final judge of the extent of the powers delegated to itself; since that would have made its discretion, and not the Constitution, the measure of its powers; but that, as in all other cases of compact among powers having no common judge, each party has an equal right to judge for itself, as well of infractions as of the mode and measure of redress.

2. *Resolved,* That the Constitution of the United States, having delegated to Congress a power to punish treason, counterfeiting the securities and current coin of the United States, piracies, and felonies committed on the high seas, and offenses against the law of nations, and no other crimes, whatsoever; and it being true as a general principle, and one of the amendments to the Constitution having also declared, that "the powers not delegated to the United States by the Constitution, not prohibited by it to the States, are reserved to the States respectively, or to the people," therefore the

act of Congress, passed on the 14th day of July, 1798, and entitled "An Act in addition to the act entitled An Act for the punishment of certain crimes against the United States," as also the act passed by them on the day of June, 1798, entitled "An Act to punish frauds committed on the bank of the United States," (and all their other acts which assume to create, define, or punish crimes, other than those so enumerated in the Constitution,) are altogether void, and of no force; and that the power to create, define, and punish such other crimes is reserved, and, of right, appertains solely and exclusively to the respective States, each within its own territory.

3. *Resolved*, That it is true as a general principle, and is also expressly declared by one of the amendments to the Constitutions, that "the powers not delegated to the United States by the Constitution, are prohibited by it to the States, are reserved to the States respectively, or to the people"; and that no power over the freedom of religion, freedom of speech, or freedom of the press being delegated to the United States by the Constitution, nor prohibited by it to the States, all lawful powers respecting the same did of right remain, and were reserved to the States or the people: that thus was manifested their determination to retain to themselves the right of judging how far the licentiousness of speech and of the press may be abridged without lessening their useful freedom, and how far those abuses which cannot be separated from their use should be tolerated, rather than the use be destroyed. And thus, also they guarded against all abridgment by the United States of the freedom of religious opinions and exercises and retained to themselves the right of protecting the same, as this State, by a law passed on the general demand of its citizens, had already protected them from all human restraint or interference. And that in addition to this general principle and express declaration, another and more special provision has been made by one of the amendments to the Constitution, which expressly declares, that "Congress shall make no law respecting an establishment of religion, or prohibiting the free exercise thereof, or abridging the freedom of speech or of the press": thereby guarding in the same sentence, and under

the same words, the freedom of religion, of speech, and of the press: insomuch, that whatever violated either, throws down the sanctuary which covers the others, arid that libels, falsehood, and defamation, equally with heresy and false religion, are withheld from the cognizance of federal tribunals. That, therefore, the act of Congress of the United States, passed on the 14th day of July 1798, entitled "An Act in addition to the act entitled An Act for the punishment of certain crimes against the United States," which does abridge the freedom of the press, is not law, but is altogether void, and of no force.

4. *Resolved*, That alien friends are under the jurisdiction and protection of the laws of the State wherein they are: that no power over them has been delegated to the United States, nor prohibited to the individual States, distinct from their power over citizens. And it being true as a general principle, and one of the amendments to the Constitution having also declared, that "the powers not delegated to the United States by the Constitution, nor prohibited by it to the States, are reserved to the States respectively, or to the people," the act of the Congress of the United States, passed on the day of July, 1798, entitled "An Act concerning aliens," which assumes powers over alien friends, not delegated by the Constitution, is not law, but is altogether void, and of no force.

5. *Resolved*. That in addition to the general principle, as well as the express declaration, that powers not delegated are reserved, another and more special provision, inserted in the Constitution from abundant caution, has declared that "the migration or importation of such persons as any of the States now existing shall think proper to admit, shall not be prohibited by the Congress prior to the year 1808" that this commonwealth does admit the migration of alien friends, described as the subject of the said act concerning aliens: that a provision against prohibiting their migration, is a provision against all acts equivalent thereto, or it would be nugatory: that to remove them when migrated, is equivalent to a prohibition of their

migration, and is, therefore, contrary to the said provision of the Constitution, and void.

6. *Resolved,* That the imprisonment of a person under the protection of the laws of this commonwealth, on his failure to obey the simple order of the President to depart out of the United States, as is undertaken by said act entitled "An Act concerning aliens" is contrary to the Constitution, one amendment to which has provided that "no person shalt be deprived of liberty without due progress of law"; and that another having provided that "in all criminal prosecutions the accused shall enjoy the right to public trial by an impartial jury, to be informed of the nature and cause of the accusation, to be confronted with the witnesses against him, to have compulsory process for obtaining witnesses in his favor, and to have the assistance of counsel for his defense;" the same act, undertaking to authorize the President to remove a person out of the United States, who is under the protection of the law, on his own suspicion, without accusation, without jury, without public trial, without confrontation of the witnesses against him, without hearing witnesses in his favor, without defense, without counsel, is contrary to the provision also of the Constitution, is therefore not law, but utterly void, and of no force: that transferring the power of judging any person, who is under the protection of the laws from the courts, to the President of the United States, as is undertaken by the same act concerning aliens, is against the article of the Constitution which provides that "the judicial power of the United States shall be vested in courts, the judges of which shall hold their offices during good behavior"; and that the said act is void for that reason also. And it is further to be noted, that this transfer of judiciary power is to that magistrate of the general government who already possesses the entire Executive, and a negative on all Legislative powers.

7. *Resolved,* That the construction applied by the General Government (as is evidenced by sundry of their proceedings) to those parts of the Constitution of the United States which delegate

to Congress a power "to lay and collect taxes, duties, imports, and excises, to pay the debts, and provide for the common defense and general welfare of the United States," and "to make all laws which shall be necessary and proper for carrying into execution, the powers vested by the Constitution in the government of the United States, or in any department or officer thereof," goes to the destruction of all limits prescribed to their powers by the Constitution: that words meant by the instrument to be subsidiary only to the execution of limited powers, ought not to be so construed as themselves to give unlimited powers, nor a part to be so taken as to destroy the whole residue of that instrument: that the proceedings of the General Government under color of these articles, will be a fit and necessary subject of revisal and correction, at a time of greater tranquility, while those specified in the preceding resolutions call for immediate redress.

8. *8th Resolved,* That a committee of conference and correspondence be appointed, who shall have in charge to communicate the preceding resolutions to the Legislatures of the several States: to assure them that this commonwealth continues in the same esteem of their friendship and union which it has manifested from that moment at which a common danger first suggested a common union: that it considers union, for specified national purposes, and particularly to those specified in their late federal compact, to be friendly, to the peace, happiness and prosperity of all the States: that faithful to that compact, according to the plain intent and meaning in which it was understood and acceded to by the several parties, it is sincerely anxious for its preservation: that it does also believe, that to take from the States all the powers of self-government and transfer them to a general and consolidated government, without regard to the special delegations and reservations solemnly agreed to in that compact, is not for the peace, happiness or prosperity of these States; and that therefore this commonwealth is determined, as it doubts not its co-States are, to submit to un-delegated, and consequently unlimited powers in no man, or body of men on earth: that in cases of an abuse

of the delegated powers, the members of the general government, being chosen by the people, a change by the people would be the constitutional remedy; but, where powers are assumed which have not been delegated, a nullification of the act is the rightful remedy: that every State has a natural right in cases not within the compact, *(casus non fœderis)* to nullify of their own authority all assumptions of power by others within their limits: that without this right, they would be under the dominion, absolute and unlimited, of whosoever might exercise this right of judgment for them: that nevertheless, this commonwealth, from motives of regard and respect for its co States, has wished to communicate with them on the subject: that with them alone it is proper to communicate, they alone being parties to the compact, and solely authorized to judge in the last resort of the powers exercised under it, Congress being not a party, but merely the creature of the compact, and subject as to its assumptions of power to the final judgment of those by whom, and for whose use itself and its powers were all created and modified: that if the acts before specified should stand, these conclusions would flow from them; that the general government may place any act they think proper on the list of crimes and punish it themselves whether enumerated or not enumerated by the constitution as cognizable by them: that they may transfer its cognizance to the President, or any other person, who may himself be the accuser, counsel, judge and jury, whose suspicions may be the evidence, his order the sentence, his officer the executioner, and his breast the sole record of the transaction: that a very numerous and valuable description of the inhabitants of these States being, by this precedent, reduced, as outlaws, to the absolute dominion of one man, and the barrier of the Constitution thus swept away from us all, no ramparts now remains against the passions and the powers of a majority in Congress to protect from a like exportation, or other more grievous punishment, the minority of the same body, the legislatures, judges, governors and counselors of the States, nor their other peaceable inhabitants, who may venture to reclaim the constitutional rights and liberties of the States and people, or who for other causes, good or bad, may be obnoxious to the views, or marked by the suspicions of the President, or be thought dangerous to his or their election, or other interests, public or personal; that the friendless alien has indeed been selected as the safest subject of a first experiment; but the citizen will soon follow, or rather, has already followed, for already has a sedition act marked him as its prey: that these and successive acts of the same character, unless arrested at the threshold, necessarily drive these States into revolution and blood and will furnish new calumnies against republican government, and new pretexts for those who wish it to be believed that man cannot be governed but by a rod of iron: that it would be a dangerous delusion were a confidence in the men of our choice to silence our fears for the safety of our rights: that confidence is everywhere the parent of despotism   free government is founded in jealousy, and not in confidence; it is jealousy and not confidence which prescribes limited constitutions, to bind down those whom we are obliged to trust with power: that our Constitution has accordingly fixed the limits to which, and no further, our confidence may go; and let the honest advocate of confidence read the Alien and Sedition acts, and say if the Constitution has not been wise in fixing limits to the government it created, and whether we should be wise in destroying those limits, Let him say what the government is, if it be not a tyranny, which the men of our choice have con erred on our President, and the President of our choice has assented to, and accepted over the friendly stranger to whom the mild spirit of our country and its law have pledged hospitality and protection: that the men of our choice have more respected the bare suspicion of the President, than the solid right of innocence, the claims of justification, the sacred force of truth, and the forms and substance of law and justice. In questions of powers, then, let no more be heard of confidence in man, but bind him down from mischief by the chains of the Constitution. That this commonwealth does therefore call on its co-States for an expression of their sentiments on the acts concerning aliens and for the punishment of certain crimes herein before specified, plainly declaring whether these acts are or are not authorized by the federal compact. And it doubts not that their sense will be so announced as to prove their attachment unaltered to limited government, weather general or particular. And that the rights and liberties of their co-States will be exposed to no dangers by remaining embarked in a common bottom with their own. That they will concur with this commonwealth in considering the said acts as so palpably against the Constitution as to amount to an undisguised declaration that that compact is not meant to be the measure of the powers of the General Government, but that it will proceed in the exercise over these States, of all powers whatsoever: that they will view this as seizing the rights of the States, and consolidating them in the hands of the General Government, with a power assumed to bind the States (not merely as the cases made federal, casus fœderis but), in all cases whatsoever, by laws made, not with their consent, but by others against their consent: that this would be to surrender the form of government we have chosen, and live under one deriving its powers from its own will, and not from our authority; and that the co-States, recurring to their natural right in cases not made federal, will concur in declaring these acts void, and of no force, and will each take measures of its own for providing that neither these acts, nor any others of the General Government not plainly and intentionally authorized by the Constitution, shalt be exercised within their respective territories.

9. 9th. Resolved, That the said committee be authorized to communicate by writing or personal conference, at any times or places whatever, with any person or persons who may be appointed by any one or more co-States to correspond or confer with them; and that they lay their proceedings before the next session of Assembly.

Virginia Resolutions of 1798
by James Madison

The Virginia Resolutions of 1798 were written secretly by James Madison in response to the <u>Alien and Sedition Acts</u> passed by the federal government. The laws were judged to be unconstitutional by Virginia and Kentucky.

Resolved, that the General Assembly of Virginia, doth unequivocally express a firm resolution to maintain and defend the Constitution of the United States, and the Constitution of this state, against every aggression, either foreign or domestic; and that they will support the government of the United States in all measures warranted by the former.

That this assembly most solemnly declares a warm attachment to the union of the states, to maintain which it pledges its powers; and that, for this end, it is their duty to watch over and oppose every infraction of those principles which constitute the only basis of that Union, because a faithful observance of them, can alone secure its existence and the public happiness.

That this Assembly doth explicitly and peremptorily declare, that it views the powers of the federal government as resulting from the compact to which the states are parties, as limited by the plain sense and intention of the instrument constituting that compact, as no further valid than they are authorized by the grants enumerated in that compact; and that, in case of a deliberate, palpable, and dangerous exercise of other powers, not granted by the said compact, the states, who are parties thereto, have the right, and are in duty bound, to interpose, for arresting the progress of the evil, and for maintaining, within their respective limits, the authorities, rights and liberties, appertaining to them.

That the General Assembly doth also express its deep regret, that a spirit has, in sundry instances, been manifested by the federal government to enlarge its powers by forced constructions of the constitutional charter which defines them; and that implications have appeared of a design to expound certain general phrases (which, having been copied from the very limited grant of power in the former Articles of Confederation, were the less liable to be misconstrued) so as to destroy the meaning and effect of the particular enumeration which necessarily explains and limits the general phrases; and so as to consolidate the states, by degrees, into one sovereignty, the obvious tendency and inevitable consequence of which would be, to transform the present republican system of the United States, into an absolute, or, at best, a mixed monarchy.

That the General Assembly doth particularly PROTEST against the palpable and alarming infractions of the Constitution, in the two late cases of the "Alien and Sedition Acts," passed at the last session of Congress; the first of which exercises a power nowhere delegated to the federal government, and which by uniting legislative and judicial powers to those of executive, subverts the general principles of free government; as well as the particular organization and positive provisions of the Federal Constitution; and the other of which acts exercises, in like manner, a power not delegated by the Constitution, but, on the contrary, expressly and positively forbidden by one of the amendments thereto, a power which more than any other, ought to produce universal alarm, because it is levelled against that right of freely examining public characters and measures, and of free communication among the people thereon, which has ever been justly deemed the only effectual guardian of every other right.

That this state having, by its Convention, which ratified the Federal Constitution, expressly declared that, among other essential rights, "the liberty of conscience and the press cannot be cancelled, abridged, restrained, or modified, by any authority of the United States," and from its extreme anxiety to guard these rights from every possible attack of sophistry and ambition, having, with other states, recommended an amendment for that purpose, which amendment was, in due time, annexed to the Constitution, it would mark a reproachable inconsistency, and criminal degeneracy, if an indifference were now shown to the most palpable violation of one of the rights thus declared and secured, and to the establishment of a precedent which may be fatal to the other.

That the good people of this commonwealth, having ever felt, and continuing to feel, the most sincere affection for their brethren of the other states; the truest anxiety for establishing and perpetuating the union of all; and the most scrupulous fidelity to that Constitution, which is the pledge of mutual friendship, and the instrument of mutual happiness, the General Assembly doth solemnly appeal to the like dispositions in the other states, in confidence that they will concur with this commonwealth in declaring, as it does hereby declare, that the acts aforesaid are unconstitutional; and that the necessary and proper measures will be taken *by each*, for cooperating with this state, in maintaining unimpaired the authorities, rights, and liberties, reserved to the states respectively, or to the people. That the Governor be desired, to transmit a copy of the foregoing resolutions to the executive authority of each of the other states, with a request that the same may be communicated to the legislature thereof, and that a copy be furnished to each of the senators and representatives representing this state in the Congress of the United States.

Attest,

JOHN STEWART

1798, December 24. Agreed to by the Senate.

H. BROOKE.

A true copy from the original deposited in the office of the General Assembly.

JOHN STEWART, *Keeper of Rolls*

The philosophy of the two resolutions:

The resolutions opposed the federal Alien and Sedition Acts, which extended the powers of the federal government. They argued that the Constitution was a "compact" or agreement among the states. Therefore, the federal government had no right to exercise powers not specifically delegated to it and that if the federal government assumed such powers, acts under them would be void. So, states could decide the constitutionality of laws passed by Congress.

A key provision of the Kentucky Resolutions was Resolution 2, which denied Congress more than a few penal powers:

That the Constitution of the United States, having delegated to Congress a power to punish treason, counterfeiting the securities and current coin of the United States, piracies, and felonies committed on the high seas, and offenses against the law of nations, and no other crimes, whatsoever; and it being true as a general principle, and one of the amendments to the Constitution having also declared, that "the powers not delegated to the United States by the Constitution, not prohibited by it to the States, are reserved to the States respectively, or to the people," therefore the act of Congress, passed on the 14th day of July, 1798, and entitled "An Act in addition to the act entitled An Act for the punishment of certain crimes against the United States," as also the act passed by them on the   day of June, 1798, entitled "An Act to punish frauds committed on the bank of the United States," (and all their other acts which assume to create, define, or punish crimes, other than those so enumerated in the Constitution,) are altogether void, and of no force; and that the power to create, define, and punish such other crimes is reserved, and, of right, appertains solely and exclusively to the respective States, each within its own territory.

The Legislative History

Thomas Jefferson wrote the Kentucky Resolutions (plural). The Kentucky state legislature passed the first resolution on November 16, 1798 and the second on December 3, 1799.

James Madison wrote the **Virginia Resolution** (singular). The Virginia state legislature passed it on December 24, 1798.

The Resolutions joined the foundational beliefs of Jefferson's party and were used as party documents in the 1800 election. As they had been shepherded to passage in the Virginia House of Delegates by John Taylor of Caroline, they became part of the heritage of the "Old Republicans." Taylor, unlike James Madison, rejoiced in what the House of Delegates had made of private citizen Madison's draft: it had read the claim that the Alien and Sedition Acts were unconstitutional as meaning that they had "no force or effect" in Virginia – that is, that they were void. Numerous scholars (including Koch and Ammon) have noted that Madison had the words "void, and of no force or effect" excised from the Resolutions before adoption. Future Virginia Governor and U.S. Secretary of War James Barbour concluded that "unconstitutional" included "void, and of no force or effect." Barbour concluded that Madison's textual change did not affect the meaning. Their long-term importance lies not in their attack on the Sedition law, but rather in their strong statements of states' rights theory, which led to rather different concepts of nullification and interposition. Jefferson at one point drafted a threat for Virginia to secede, but dropped it from the text. In January 1800, the Virginia General Assembly passed the Report of 1800, a document by Madison affirming the principles of the Resolutions and responding to criticism they had received.

The resolutions were submitted to the other states for approval but with no success. In New Hampshire, newspapers treated them as military threats and replied with foreshadowing's of civil war. "We think it highly probable that Virginia and Kentucky will be sadly disappointed in their infernal plan of exciting insurrections and tumults," proclaimed one. The state legislature's unanimous reply was blunt:

"Resolved that the Legislature of New Hampshire unequivocally express a firm resolution to maintain and defend the Constitution of the United States, and the Constitution of this State against every aggression either foreign or domestic, and that they will support the Government of the United States in all measures warranted by the former. That the State Legislatures are not the proper tribunals to determine the Constitutionality of the laws of the General Government that the duty of such decision is properly and exclusively confided to the Judicial department."

Alexander Hamilton, then building up the army, suggested sending it into Virginia, on some "obvious pretext." Measures would be taken, Hamilton hinted to an ally in Congress, "to act upon the laws and put Virginia to the Test of resistance."

All the New England states rejected the resolutions. However, the state governments of Massachusetts, Connecticut, and Rhode Island threatened to ignore the Embargo Act of 1807 based on the authority of states to stand up to laws deemed by those states to be unconstitutional. Rhode Island justified its position on the embargo act based on the explicit language of interposition. Within five years, Massachusetts and Connecticut asserted their right to test constitutionality when instructed to send their militias to defend the coast during the War of 1812. Connecticut and Massachusetts questioned another embargo passed in 1813. The supreme courts of both states objected, including this statement from the Massachusetts General Court:

During the "nullification crisis" of 1828-1833, South Carolina threatened to nullify a federal law regarding tariffs. Andrew Jackson issued a proclamation against the doctrine of nullification, stating: "I consider...the power to annul a law of the United States, assumed by one State, incompatible with the existence of the Union, contradicted expressly by the letter of the Constitution, unauthorized by its spirit, inconsistent with every principle on which it was founded, and destructive of the great object for which it was formed." He also denied the right to secede: "The Constitution...forms a government not a league...To say that any State may at pleasure secede from the Union is to say that the United States is not a nation." Later, Abraham Lincoln also rejected the compact theory saying the Constitution was a binding contract among the states and no contract can be changed unilaterally by one party.

In 2009, Dan Itse, a member of the New Hampshire House of Representatives from Fremont, New Hampshire, led a national movement to restore the powers of the states through the Kentucky and Virginia Resolutions.

Chapter 3

Davy Crockett See's the Light

A Turing Point for One Congressman

Turning Points

From the words of Edward S. Ellis:

"As a coonskin-capped Disney legend, Davy Crockett captured the imagination of several generations of American youth. But in real life, before he was a hero at the Alamo, Crockett was a U.S. Congressman from Tennessee – from 1827 to 1833. The following classic story, reprinted from the 1884 book "The Life of Colonel David Crockett" compiled by Edward S. Ellis (Philadelphia: Porter & Coates), illustrates perfectly the root cause of Congress's unconstitutional and ever-expanding taxing and spending, as well as the best and only true solution."

One day in the House of Representatives a bill was taken up appropriating money for the benefit of a widow of a distinguished naval officer. Several beautiful speeches had been made in its support. The speaker was just about to put the question when Crockett arose:

"Mr. Speaker – I have as much respect for the memory of the deceased, and as much sympathy for the suffering of the living, if there be, as any man in the House, but we must not permit our respect for the dead or our sympathy for part of the living to lead us into an act of injustice to the balance of the living. I will not go into an argument to prove that Congress has not the power to appropriate this money as an act of charity. Every member on this floor knows it.

"We have the right, as individuals, to give away as much of our own money as we please in charity; but as members of Congress, we have no right to appropriate a dollar of the public money. Some eloquent appeals have been made to us upon the ground that is a debt due to the deceased. Mr. Speaker, the deceased lived long after the close of the war; he was in office to the day of his death, and I never heard that the government was in arrears to him."

"Every man in this House knows it is not a debt. We cannot without the grossest corruption, appropriate this money as the payment of a debt. We have not the semblance of authority to appropriate it as charity. Mr. Speaker, I have said we have the right to give as much money of our own as we please. I am the poorest man on the floor. I cannot vote for this bill, but I will give one week's pay to the object, and if every member of Congress will do the same, it will amount to more than the bill asks."

He took his seat. Nobody replied. The bill was put upon its passage, and instead of passing unanimously, as was generally supposed, and as no doubt it would but for that speech, it received but few votes and, of course, was lost.

Later, when asked by a friend why he had opposed the appropriation, Crockett gave this explanation:

"Several years ago, I was one evening standing on the steps of the Capitol with some members of Congress, when our attention was attracted by a great light over in Georgetown. It was evidently a large fire. We jumped into a hack and drove over as fast as we could. In spite of all that could be done, many houses, some of them had lost all but the clothes they had on. The weather was very cold, and when I saw so many children suffering, I felt that something ought to be done for them. The next morning a bill was introduced appropriating $20,000.00 for their relief. We put aside all other business and rushed it through as soon as it could be done."

"The Next summer, when it began to be time to think about election, I concluded I would take a scout around among the boys of my district. I had no opposition there but, as the election was some time off, I did not know what might turn up. When riding one day in a part of my district in which I was more of a stranger than any other, I saw a man in a field plowing and coming toward the road. I gauged my gait so that we should meet as he came up, I spoke to the man. He replied politely, but as I thought, rather coldly.

"I began: 'Well friend, I am one of those unfortunate beings called candidates and

"Yes I know you; you are Colonel Crockett. I have seen you once before and voted for you the last time you were elected. I suppose you are out electioneering now, but you had better not waste your time or mine, I shall not vote for you again.

"This was a sockdolager ... I begged him tell me what the matter was.

"Well Colonel, it is hardly worthwhile to waste time or words upon it. I do not see how it can be mended, but you gave a vote last winter which shows that either you have not capacity to understand the Constitution, or that you are wanting in the honesty and firmness to be guided by it. In either case you are not the man to represent me. But I beg your pardon for expressing it that way. I did not intend to avail myself of the privilege of the constituent to speak plainly to a candidate for the purpose of insulting you or wounding you. I intend by it only so say that your understanding of the Constitution is very different from mine; and I will say to you what but for my rudeness, I should not have said, that I believe you to be honest... But an understanding of the Constitution different from mine I cannot overlook, because the Constitution, to be worth anything, must be held sacred, and rigidly observed in all its provisions. The man who wields power and misinterprets it is the more dangerous the more honest he is.'

"'I admit the truth of all you say, but there must be some mistake about it, for I do not remember that I gave any vote last winter upon any constitutional question.'

"'No, Colonel, there's no mistake. Though I live in the backwoods and seldom go from home, I take the papers from Washington and read very carefully all the proceedings of Congress. My papers say you voted for a bill to appropriate $20,000 to some sufferers by fire in Georgetown. Is that true?'

"'Well, my friend, I may as well own up. You have got me there. But certainly, nobody will complain that a great and rich country like ours should give the insignificant sum of $20,000 to relieve its suffering women and children, particularly with a full and overflowing treasury, and I am sure, if you had been there, you would have done just the same as I did.

"'It is not the amount, Colonel, that I complain of; it is the principle. In the first place, the government ought to have in the Treasury no more than enough for its legitimate purposes. But that has nothing to do with the question. The power of collecting and disbursing money at pleasure is the most dangerous power that can be entrusted to man, particularly under our system of collecting revenue by a tariff, which reaches every man in the country, no matter how poor he may be, and the poorer he is the more he pays in proportion to his means.

"'*What is worse, it presses upon him without his knowledge where the weight centers, for there is not a man in the United States who can ever guess how much he pays to the government. So, you see that while you are contributing to relieve one, you are drawing it from thousands who are even worse off than he. If you had the right to give anything, the amount was simply a matter of discretion with you, and you had as much right to give $20,000,000 as $20,000. If you have the right to give to one, you have the right to give to all; and as the Constitution neither defines charity nor stipulates the amount, you are at liberty to give to any and everything which you may believe, or profess to believe, is a charity and to any amount you may think proper. You will very easily perceive what a wide door this* would open for fraud and corruption and favoritism on the one hand, and for _robbing_ the people on the other.

"'No, Colonel, Congress has no right to give charity. Individual members may give as much of their money as they please, but they have no right to touch a dollar of the public money for that purpose. If twice as many houses had been burned in this county as in Georgetown, neither you nor any other member of Congress would have thought of appropriating a dollar for our relief. There are about two hundred and forty members of Congress. If they had shown their sympathy for the sufferers by contributing each one week's pay, it would have made over $13,000. There are plenty of wealthy men around Washington who could have given $20,000 without depriving themselves of even a luxury of life. The congressmen chose to keep their money, which, if reports be true, some of them spend not very creditably; and for relieving them from the necessity of giving what was not yours to give. The people have delegated to Congress, by the Constitution, the power to do certain things. To do these, it is authorized to collect and pay moneys, and for nothing else. Everything beyond this is usurpation, and a violation of the Constitution.

"So you see, Colonel, you have violated the Constitution in what I consider a vital point. It is a precedent fraught with danger to the country, for when Congress once begins to stretch its power beyond the limits of the Constitution, there is no limit to it and no security for the people. I have no doubt you acted honestly, but that does not make it any better, except as far as you are personally concerned, and you see that I cannot vote for you."'I tell you I felt streaked. I saw if I should have opposition, and this man should go to talking, he would set other to talking, and in the district, I was a gone fawn-skin. I could not answer him, and the fact is, I was so fully convinced that he was right, I did not want to. But I must satisfy him, and I said to him:

"'Well, friend, you hit the nail upon the head when you said I had not sense enough to understand the Constitution. I intended to be guided by it and thought I had studied it fully. I have heard many speeches in Congress about the powers of Congress, but what you have said here at your plow has got harder, sound sense in it than all the fine speeches I ever heard. If I had ever taken the view of it that you have, I would have put my head into the fire before I would have given that vote; and if you would forgive me and vote for me again, if I ever vote for another unconstitutional law, I wish I may be shot.'

"He laughingly replied: "Yes, Colonel, you have sworn to that once before, but I will trust you again upon one condition...

You are convinced that your vote was wrong. Your acknowledgment of it will do more good than beating you for it. If, as you go around the district, you will tell people about this vote, and that you are satisfied it was wrong, I will not only vote for you, but will do what I can to keep down opposition, and perhaps, I may exert some little influence in the way.'

"'If I don't, said I, I wish I may be shot; and to convince you that I am in earnest in what I say I will come back this way in a week or ten days, and if you will get up a gathering of people, I will make a speech to them. Get up a barbecue, and I will pay for it.'

"'No, Colonel, we are not rich people in this section but we have plenty of provisions to contribute for a barbecue, and some to spare for those who have none. The push of crops will be over in a few days, and we can then afford a day for a barbecue. This is Thursday; I will see to getting it up on Saturday week. Come to my house on Friday, and we will go together, and I promise you a very respectable crowd to see and hear you.'

"Well, I will be here. But one thing more before I say goodbye, I must know your name".

"My name is Bunce". "Not Horatio Bunce"? "'Yes".

"'Well, Mr. Bunce, I never saw you before, though you say you have seen me, but I know you very well. I am glad I have met you, and very proud that I may hope to have you for my friend".

"It was one of the luckiest hits of my life that I met him. He mingled but little with the public but was widely known for his remarkable intelligence and for a heart brim-full and running over with kindness and benevolence, which showed themselves not only in words but in acts. He was the oracle of the whole country around him, and his fame had extended for beyond the circle of his immediate acquaintance. Though I had never met him before, I had heard much of him, and but for this meeting it is very likely I should have had opposition and had been beaten. One thing certain; no man could now stand up in that district under such a vote.

"At the appointed time I was at his house, having told our conversation to every crowd I had met, and to every man I stayed all night with, and I found that it gave the people an interest and confidence in me stronger than I had ever seen manifested before.

"Though I was considerably fatigued when I reached his house, and, under ordinary circumstances, should have gone early to bed, I kept him up until midnight talking about the principles and affairs of government, and got more real, true knowledge of them than I had got all my life before.

"I have known and seen much of him since, for I respect him – no, that is not the word – I reverence and love him more than any living man, and I go to see him two or three times every year; and I will tell you sir, if everyone who professes to be a Christian lived and acted and enjoyed it as he does, the religion of Christ would take the world by storm.

"But to return to my story, the next morning we went to the barbecue and, to my surprise, found about a thousand men there. I met a good many whom I had not know before, and they and my friend introduced me around until I had got pretty well acquainted – at least, they all knew me.

"In due time notice was given that I would speak to them. They gathered up around a stand that had been erected. I opened my speech by saying:

"'Fellow-citizens – I present myself before you today feeling like a new man. My eyes have lately been opened to truths which ignorance or prejudice or both had heretofore hidden from my view. I feel that I can today offer you

the ability to render you more valuable service than I have ever been able to render before. I am here today more for the purpose of acknowledging my error than to seek your votes. That I should make this acknowledgment is due to myself as well as to you. Whether you will vote for me is a matter for your consideration only.'

"*I went on to tell them about the fire and my vote for the appropriation and told them why I was satisfied it was wrong. I led by saying:*

"'*And now, fellow-citizens, it remains only for me to tell you that most of the speech you have listened to with so much interest was simply a repetition of the arguments by which your neighbor, Mr. Bunce, convinced me of my error. It is the best speech I ever made in my life, but he is entitled to the credit for it. And Now I hope he is satisfied with his convert and he will get up here and tell you so.'*

"*He came up to the stand and said:*

"'*Fellow citizens, it affords me great pleasure to comply with the request of Colonel Crockett. I have always considered him a thoroughly honest man and I am satisfied that he will faithfully perform all that he has promised you today.*"

"*He went down, and there went up from that crowd such a shout for Davy Crockett as his name never called forth before.*"

"*I am not much given to tears, but I was taken with a choking then and felt some big drops rolling down my cheeks. And I tell you now that the remembrance of those few words spoken by such a man, and the honest, hearty shout they produced, is worth more to me than all the honors I have received and all the reputation I have ever made, or ever shall make, as a member of Congress.'*

"*Now, sir,*" *concluded Crockett,* "*you know why I made that speech yesterday.*"

"There is one thing now to which I will call your attention. You remember that I proposed to give a week's pay. There are in that House many very wealthy men – men who think nothing of spending a week's pay, or a dozen of them, for a dinner or a wine party when they have something to accomplish by it. Some of those same men made beautiful speeches upon the great debt of gratitude which the country owed the deceased – a debt which could not be paid by money – and the insignificance and worthlessness of money, particularly so insignificant a sum as $20,000 when weighed against the honor of the nation. Yet not one then, responded to my proposition. Money with them is nothing but trash when it is to come out of the people. But it is the one great thing for which most of them are striving, and many of them sacrifice honor, integrity, and justice to obtain it."

Edward Sylvester Ellis – born April 11, 1840, died June 20, 1916 – was an American author best known for his Deer Hunter novels and other classic westerns.

To all that read this small but important part of our history, regarding Davy Crockett, I hope the meaning of his thoughts will dwell deep into the hearts and spirits of Americans and those that are given the task to represent the People in Congress.

Chapter 4

The Progressive Movement in America

An Anathema of Liberty and Christianity

*Redacted from the Progressive Movement and the Transformation of American Politics
Remarks by Thomas G. West and Commentary by William A. Schambra

Secular Progressivism (Statists, Socialism, Communism, and Liberalism) is a reform movement that began in the late 19th century. When I speak of Progressivism, I refer to the movement that rose to prominence between about 1880 and 1920.

During this period many pseudo intellectuals and misguided social reformers in the United States sought to address the economic, political, and social issues of the day that had arisen as a result of the rapid changes brought with the Industrial Revolution, WW I, the Depression and the growth of modern capitalism in America.

The Progressives fallaciously believed that these events marked the end of the old order of the Founders and required the creation of a new order more appropriate for the new industrial age.

While the Progressives differed in their assessment of the problems and how to resolve them, they generally shared in common the view that a vastly expanded and empowered government must at every level of society be actively involved in forcing these reforms.

The Progressives felt the existing constitutional system was outdated and that it must be <u>made into a dynamic, evolving instrument of social change, aided by the</u> accelerated development of administrative Government bureaucracy.

At the same time, the Progressives pushed for the old system to be scraped and made more democratic; hence, the direct elections of Senators, the open primary, the initiative and referendum.

The expanded government was expensive and had to be provided for; hence, the Sixteenth Amendment and the progressive income tax were implemented to raise revenues to feed the bloated and ever expanding Government Monster.

What was the Progressive transformation? It was a total rejection in theory, and a partial rejection in practice, of the principles and policies on which America had been founded and which had been working so well since the Foundation.

Today, those who speak of the formative influences that made America what it is today, tend to endorse one of three main explanations. Some emphasize material factors such as the closing of the frontier, the Industrial Revolution, the rise of the modern corporation, and accidental emergencies such as wars or the Great Depression, which in turn led to the rise of the modern administrative state.

Second is the rational explanation of choices. Once government became involved in providing extensive services for the public, politicians saw that the growth in government programs enabled them to win elections.

The politicians quickly realized that the more government does, the easier it is for Congressmen to do favors for voters and donors and thus garner votes…sort of a Quid Pro Quo…

Third, still other scholars believe that the ideas of the American founding itself are responsible for current developments.

The Progressives claim that the Founders themselves did not understand the implications of the ideas of the Revolution, and that those ideas eventually "made possible…all our current egalitarian thinking."

My own view is this: Although the first two of the three mentioned causes (material circumstances and politicians' self-interest) certainly played a part, the most important cause was a change in the prevailing understanding of justice among leading American intellectuals and, to a lesser extent, in the American people.

Today's liberalism and the policies that it has spawned arose from a conscious repudiation of the principles of the America's Founders.

The Progressive Revolutionaries are entirely wrong in their claim that contemporary liberalism is a logical outgrowth of the principles of the Founding. It is not…

During the Progressive Era, a new theory of justice took hold. Its power has been so great that.

Progressivism, as modified by later developments within contemporary liberalism, has become the predominant view in modern American education, media, Hollywood, and Leftist politics. Today, people who call themselves conservatives and liberals alike recognize the Progressive's tortured view of the world.

1. The Progressive Rejection of the Founding

Shortly after the end of the Civil War, a large majority of Americans shared a set of beliefs concerning the purpose of government, its structure, and most important its public policies. Constitutional amendments were passed abolishing slavery and giving the national government the authority to protect the basic civil rights of everyone. Here was a legal foundation on which the promise of the American Revolution could be realized in the South, beyond its already existing implementation in the Northern and Western states.

This post–Civil War consensus was animated by the principles of America's Founders. Between about 1880 and 1920, the earlier Founder's orientation gradually began to be replaced by the new Progressive one.

In FDR's New Deal period of the 1930s, and later even more decisively in LBJ's War on Poverty in the 1960s and '70s lay the impetus for an expanded impact of the Federal Government on everyday life. The Progressive view, increasingly radicalized by its transformation into contemporary liberalism, became a very powerful albeit a small but very loud organized and well-funded militant minority emerged on to the National stage.

2. The Rejection of Nature and the Turn to History

The Founders believed that all men are created equal and that they have certain inalienable rights. All are also obliged to obey the natural law, under which we have not only rights but duties.

We are obliged "to respect those rights in others which we value in ourselves." (Jefferson).

The main rights were thought to be life and liberty, including the liberty to organize one's own church, to associate at work or at home with whomever one pleases, and to use one's talents to acquire and keep property. For the Founders, then, there is a natural moral order rules discovered by human reason that promote human well-being, rules that can and should guide human life and politics.

The Progressives categorically rejected these claims as naive and unhistorical.

In their revisionist view, human beings are not born free. John Dewey, the most thoughtful of the Progressives, wrote that freedom is not "something that individuals have as a ready-made possession." It is "something to be achieved." In this view, freedom is not a gift of God or nature. It is a product of human making, a gift of the state.

Man is a product of his own history, through which he collectively creates himself. He is thus a social construct.

Since, according to Progressive thinking, human beings are not naturally free, there can be no natural rights or natural law.

Therefore, Dewey also writes, "Natural rights and natural liberties exist only in the kingdom of mythological social zoology."

Since the Progressives held that nature gives man little or nothing and that everything of value to human life is made by man, they concluded that there are no permanent standards of right. Dewey spoke of "historical relativity." However, in one sense, the Progressives did believe that human beings are oriented toward freedom, not by nature (which, is a merely primitive process, contains nothing human), but by the historical process, which has the character of progressing toward increasing freedom.

So, the "relativity" in question means that in all times, people have views of right and wrong that are tied to their particular times, but in our time, the views of the most enlightened are true because they are in conformity with where history is going.

For the Founders, thinking about government began with the recognition that what man is given by nature his capacity for reason and the moral law discovered by reason is, in the most important respect, more valuable than anything government can give him.

Not that nature provides him with his needs. In fact, the Founders thought that civilization is indispensable for human well-being. Although government can be a threat to liberty, government is also necessary for the security of liberty and to prevent chaos.

As Madison wrote, "If men were angels, no government would be necessary." But since men are not angels, *without government, human beings would live in "a state of nature, where the weaker individual is not secured against the violence of the stronger." This has been adequately demonstrated in the recent riots where the system broke down and in the issuing chaos the rights (property and freedom) of individuals could not be protected against the power of the rioting mob....*

In the Founders' view, nature does give human beings the most valuable things: their bodies and minds. These are the basis of their talents, which they achieve by cultivating these natural gifts but which would be impossible without those gifts from God...

For the Founders, then, the individual's existence and freedom in this crucial respect are not a gift of government. They are a gift of God and nature.
Government is therefore always and fundamentally in the service of the Individual, not the other way around.

The purpose of government, then, is to enforce Natural law for the members of the political community by securing the people's natural rights.

Government does so by preserving their lives and liberties against the violence of others. In the Founding, the liberties to be secured by government are not freedom from necessity or poverty. But freedom from the despotic and predatory domination of some human beings over others, in short the prevention of tyranny.
Government's main duty according to the Founders is to secure that freedom at home through the making and enforcement of criminal and civil law, abroad through a strong national defense, through secure borders and freedom from terrorists. The protection of life and liberty is achieved through vigorous prosecutions of crime against person and property or through civil suits for recovery of damages, these cases being decided by a jury of one's peers.

The Progressives regarded the Founders' scheme as defective because it took too benign a view of nature. They thought that the individual was ready-made by nature. *The Founders' supposed failure to recognize the crucial role of society led the Progressives to disparage the Founders' insistence on limited government.*

The Progressive goal of politics is freedom, now understood as freedom from the limits imposed by nature and necessity. They rejected the Founders' conception of freedom as useful for self-preservation for the sake of the individual pursuit of happiness. *For the Progressives, freedom is redefined as the fulfillment of human capacities, which becomes the primary task of the state (Government).*

To this end, Dewey writes, *"the state has the responsibility for creating institutions under which individuals can effectively realize the potentialities that are theirs."* So, although "it is true that social arrangements, laws, institutions are made for man, rather than that man is made for them," these laws and institutions "are not means for obtaining something for individuals, not even happiness. They are means of creating individuals…. Individuality in a social and moral sense is something to be wrought out."

"Creating individuals" versus "protecting individuals": this sums up the difference between the Founders' and the Progressives' conception of what government is for.

3. The Progressives' Rejection of Consent and Compact as the Basis of Society

In accordance with their conviction that all human beings are by nature free, the Founders taught that political society is "formed by a voluntary association of individuals: It is a social compact, by which the whole people covenant with each citizen, and each citizen with the whole people, that all shall be governed by certain laws for the common good" (Massachusetts Constitution of 1780).

For the Founders, the consent principle extended beyond the founding of society into its ordinary operation. Government was to be conducted under laws, and *laws were to be made by locally elected officials, accountable through frequent elections to those who chose them. The people would be directly involved in governing through their participation in juries selected by lot.*

The Progressives treated the social compact idea with scorn. Charles Merriam, a leading Progressive political scientist, wrote:

The individualistic ideas of the "natural right" school of political theory, indorsed in the Revolution, are discredited and repudiated.... The origin of the state is regarded, not as the result of a deliberate agreement among men, but as the result of historical development, instinctive rather than conscious; and rights are considered to have their source not in nature, but in law.

For the Progressives, then, it was of no great importance whether or not government begins in consent as long as it serves its proper end of remolding man in such a way as to bring out his real capacities and aspirations.

As Merriam wrote, "it was the idea of the state that supplanted the social contract as the ground of political right." Democracy and consent are not absolutely rejected by the Progressives, but their importance is greatly diminished, as we will see when we come to the Progressive conception of governmental structure.

4. God and Religion

In the founding, God was conceived in one of two ways. Christians and Jews believed in the God of the Bible as the author of liberty but also as the author of the moral law by which human beings are guided toward their duties and, ultimately, toward their happiness.

Nonbelievers (President Washington called them "mere politicians" in his Farewell Address) thought of God merely as a creative principle or force behind the natural order of things.

Both sides agreed that there is a God of nature who endows men with natural rights and assigns them duties under the law of nature. Believers added that the God of nature is also the God of the Bible, while secular thinkers denied that God was anything more than the God of nature. Everyone saw liberty as a "sacred cause."

At least some of the Progressives redefined God as human freedom achieved through the right political organization. Or else God was simply rejected as a myth.

For Hegel, whose philosophy strongly influenced the Progressives, "the state is the divine idea as it exists on earth."

John Burgess, a prominent Progressive political scientist, wrote that the purpose of the **state** is the "perfection of humanity, the civilization of the world; the perfect development of the human reason and its attainment to universal command over individualism; the apotheosis of man" (man becoming God).

Progressive- Era theologians like Walter Rauschenbusch Redefined Christianity as the social gospel of progress.

5. Limits on Government and the Integrity of the Private Sphere

For the Founders, the purpose of government is to protect the private sphere, which they regarded as the proper home of both the high and the low, of the important and the merely urgent, of God, religion, and science, as well as providing for the needs of the body.

The experience of religious persecution had convinced the Founders that government was incompetent at directing man in his highest endeavors. The requirements of liberty, they thought, meant that self-interested private associations had to be permitted, not because they are good in themselves, but because depriving individuals of freedom of association would deny the liberty that is necessary for the health of society and the flourishing of the individual.

For the Founders, although government was grounded in divine law (i.e., the laws of nature and of nature's God), government was seen as a merely human thing, bound up with all the strengths and weaknesses of human nature. Government had to be limited both because it was dangerous if it got too powerful and because it was not supposed to provide for the highest things in life.

Because of the Progressives' tendency to view the state as divine and the natural as low, they no longer looked upon the private sphere as that which was to be protected by government. Instead, the realm of the private was seen as the realm of selfishness and oppression. Private property was especially singled out for criticism. Some Progressives openly or covertly spoke of themselves as socialists.

Progressives feel that government of this kind is unjust because it leaves men at the mercy of predatory corporations. Without government management of those corporations, Wilson thought, the poor would be destined to indefinite victimization by the wealthy. Previous limits on government power must be abolished. Accordingly, Progressive political scientist Theodore Woolsey wrote, "The sphere of the state may reach as far as the nature and needs of man and of men reach, including intellectual and aesthetic wants of the individual, and the religious and moral nature of its citizens."

However, this transformation is still in the future, for Progress takes place through historical development. A sign of the Progressives' unlimited trust in unlimited political authority is Dewey's remark in his:

"Ethics of Democracy" that Plato's Republic presents us with the "perfect man in the perfect state." What Plato's Socrates had presented as a thought experiment to expose the nature and limits of political life is taken by Dewey to be a laudable obliteration of the private sphere by government mandate. In a remark that the Founders would have found repugnant, Progressive political scientist John Burgess wrote that "the most fundamental and indispensable mark of statehood" was "the original, absolute, unlimited, universal power over the individual subject, and all associations of subjects."

6. Domestic Policy

For the Founders, domestic policy, as we have seen, concentrated on securing the persons and properties of the people against violence by means of a tough criminal law against murder, rape, robbery, and so on. Further, the civil law had to provide for the poor to have access to acquiring property by allowing the buying and selling of labor and property through voluntary contracts and a legal means of establishing undisputed ownership. The burden of proof was on government if there was to be any limitation on the free use of that property.

Thus, licensing and zoning were rare. Laws regulating sexual conduct aimed at the

formation of lasting marriages so that children would be born and provided for by those whose interest and love was most likely to lead to their proper care, with minimal government involvement needed because most families would be intact.

Finally, the Founders tried to promote the moral conditions of an independent, hard-working citizenry by laws and educational institutions that would encourage such virtues as honesty, moderation, justice, patriotism, courage, frugality, and industry. Government support of religion (typically generic Protestantism) was generally practiced with a view to these ends.

One can see the Founders' view of the connection between religion and morality in such early laws as the Northwest Ordinance of 1787, which said that government should promote education because "religion, morality, and knowledge [are] necessary to good government and the happiness of mankind."

In Progressivism, the domestic policy of government had two main concerns.

First, government must protect the poor and other victims of capitalism *through redistribution of wealth and resources,* anti-trust laws, government control over the details of commerce and production: i.e., dictating at what prices things must be sold, methods of manufacture, government participation in the banking system, and so on.

Second, government must become involved in the "spiritual" development of its citizens not, of course, through promotion of religion, but through protecting the environment ("conservation"), education (understood as education to personal creativity), and spiritual uplift through subsidy and promotion of the arts and culture.

7. Foreign Policy

For the Founders, foreign and domestic policies were supposed to serve the same end: the security of the people in their person and property. Therefore, foreign policy was conceived primarily as defensive. Foreign attack was to be deterred by having strong arms or repulsed by force. Alliances were to be entered into with the understanding that a self-governing nation must keep itself aloof from the quarrels of other nations, except as needed for national defense.

Government had no right to spend the taxes or lives of its own citizens to spread democracy to other nations or to engage in enterprises aiming at imperialistic hegemony.

The Progressives believed that a historical process was leading all mankind to freedom, or at least the advanced nations. Following Hegel, they thought of the march of freedom in history as having a geographical basis. It was in Europe, not Asia or Africa, where modern science and the modern state had made their greatest advances. The nations where modern science had properly informed the political order were thought to be the proper leaders of the world.

The Progressives also believed that the scientifically educated leaders of the advanced nations (especially America, Britain, and France) should not hesitate to rule the less advanced nations in the interest of ultimately bringing the world into freedom, assuming that supposedly inferior peoples could be brought into the modern world at all. Political scientist Charles Merriam openly called for a policy of colonialism on a racial basis:

[T]he Teutonic races must civilize the politically uncivilized. They must have a colonial policy.

Barbaric races, if incapable, may be swept away.... On the same principle, interference with the affairs of states not wholly barbaric, but nevertheless incapable of effecting political organization for them, is fully justified.

Progressives therefore embraced a much more active and indeed imperialistic foreign policy than the Founders did.

In "Expansion and Peace" (1899), Theodore Roosevelt wrote that the best policy is imperialism on a global scale: "every expansion of a great civilized power means a victory for law, order, and righteousness." Thus, the American occupation of the Philippines, T.R. believed, would enable "one more fair spot of the world's surface" to be "snatched from the forces of darkness. Fundamentally the cause of expansion is the cause of peace."

Woodrow Wilson advocated American entry into World War I, boasting that America's national interest had nothing to do with it. Wilson had no difficulty sending American troops to die in order to make the world safe for democracy, regardless of whether or not it would make America safer or less. The trend to turn power over to multinational organizations also begins in this period, as may be seen in Wilson's plan for a League of Nations, under whose rules America would have delegated control over the deployment of its own armed forces to that body.

8. Who Should Rule, Experts or Representatives?

The Founders thought that laws should be made by a body of elected officials with roots in local communities. They should not be "experts," but they should have "most wisdom to discern, and most virtue to pursue, the common good of the society" (Madison).

The wisdom in question was the kind on display in The Federalist, which relentlessly dissected the political errors of the previous decade in terms accessible to any person of intelligence and common sense.

The Progressives wanted to sweep away what they regarded as this amateurism in politics. They had confidence that modern science had superseded the perspective of the liberally educated statesman. Only those educated in the top universities, preferably in the social sciences, were thought to be capable of governing. Politics was regarded as too complex for common sense to cope with. Government had taken on the vast responsibility not merely of protecting the people against injuries, but of managing the entire economy as well as providing for the people's spiritual wellbeing.

Only government agencies staffed by experts informed by the most advanced modern science could manage tasks previously handled within the private sphere. Government, it was thought, needed to be led by those who see where history is going, who understand the ever-evolving idea of human dignity.

The Progressives did not intend to abolish democracy, to be sure. They wanted the people's will to be more efficiently translated into government policy.

But what democracy meant for the Progressives is that the people would take power out of the hands of locally elected officials and political parties and place it instead into the hands of the central government, which would in turn establish administrative agencies run by neutral experts, scientifically trained, to translate the people's inchoate will into concrete policies.

Local politicians would be replaced by neutral city managers presiding over technically trained staffs. Politics in the sense of favoritism and self-interest would disappear and be replaced by the universal rule of enlightened bureaucracy.

Progressivism and Today's Liberalism

Most obviously, the roots of the liberalism with which we are familiar lie in the Progressive Era. It is not hard to see the connections between the eight features of Progressivism.

This is true not only for the New Deal period of FDR, but above all for the major institutional and policy changes that were initiated in LBJ's War on Poverty and Civil Rights Legislation between 1965 and 1975. Whether one regards the transformation of American politics over the past century as good or bad, the foundations of that transformation were laid in the Progressive Era. Today's liberals, or the teachers of today's liberals, learned to reject the principles of the Founders from their teachers, the Progressives. Nevertheless, in some respects, the Progressives were closer to the Founders than they are to today's Liberalism.

So let us conclude by briefly considering the differences between our current Liberalism and Progressivism.

We may sum up these differences in three words: science, sex, and progress.

First, in regard to science, today's liberals have a far more ambivalent attitude than the Progressives did. The latter had no doubt that science either had all the answers or was on the road to discovering them.

Today, although the prestige of science remains great, it has been greatly diminished by the multicultural perspective that sees science as just another point of view.

So, science is just a Western perspective on reality, no more or less valid than the folk magic believed in by an African or Pacific Island tribe that has never been exposed to modern science.

Second, liberalism today has become preoccupied with sex. Sexual activity is to be freed from all traditional restraints.

In the Founders' view, sex was something that had to be regulated by government because of its tie to the production and rising of children. Practices such as abortion and homosexual conduct the choice for which was recently equated by the Supreme Court with the right "to define one's own concept of existence, of meaning, of the universe, and of the mystery of human life" are considered fundamental rights.

The connection between sexual liberation and Progressivism is indirect, for the Progressives, who tended to follow Hegel in such matters, were rather old- fashioned in this regard. But there was one premise within Progressivism that may be said to have led to the current liberal understanding of sex. That is the disparagement of nature and the celebration of human will, the idea that everything of value in life is created by man's choice, not by nature or necessity.

Once sexual conduct comes under the scrutiny of such a concern, it is not hard to see that limiting sexual expression to marriage where it is clearly tied to nature's concern for reproduction could easily be seen as a kind of limitation of human liberty.

Once self realization (Dewey's term, for whom it was still tied to reason and science) is transmuted into self-expression (today's term), all barriers to one's sexual idiosyncrasies must appear arbitrary and tyrannical.

Third, contemporary liberals no longer believe in progress. The Progressives' faith in progress was rooted in their faith in science, as one can see especially in the European thinkers whom they admired, such as Hegel and Comte. When science is seen as just one perspective among many, then progress itself comes into question.

The idea of progress presupposes that the end result is superior to the point of departure, but contemporary liberals are generally wary of expressing any sense of the superiority of the West, whether intellectually, politically, or in any other way. They are therefore disinclined to support any foreign policy venture that contributes to the strength of America or of the West.

Liberal domestic policy follows the same principle. It tends to elevate the "other" to moral superiority over against those whom the Founders would have called the decent and the honorable, the men of wisdom and virtue. The more a person is lacking, the greater is his or her moral claim on society. The deaf, the blind, the disabled, the stupid, the improvident, the ignorant, and even (in a 1984 speech of presidential candidate Walter Mondale) the sad those who are lowest are extolled as the sacred other.

Surpisingly, although Progressivism, supplemented by the more recent liberalism, has transformed America in some respects, the Founders' approach to politics is still alive in most areas of American life. One has merely to attend a jury trial over a murder, rape, robbery, or theft in a state court to see the older system of the rule of law at work. Perhaps this is one reason why America seems so conservative to the rest of the Western world.

Among ordinary Americans, as opposed to the political, academic, professional, and entertainment elites, there is still a strong attachment to property rights, self- reliance, and heterosexual marriage; a wariness of university-certified "experts"; and an unapologetic willingness to use armed forces in defense of their country.

The first great battle for the American soul was settled in the Civil War. The second battle for America's soul, initiated over a century ago, is still raging on. The choice for the Founders' constitutionalism or the Progressive- liberal administrative state is yet to be fully resolved.

The war for America's Soul still rages on. The advent of the Tea Party Movement has erected an effective barrier to the designs of the Progressive movement.
Essentially the war is between the Traditional Conservative and the Revisionist Progressives.

The focus of one to return to the values of the Founders and the Common Man, and the focus of the other to subvert America to the values of a wealthy oligarchy composed of pseudo intellectual elitists like George Soros, the evil, ruthless puppet master holding Obama's strings…

Chapter 5

The Power of the Government

The beginning of the turnover by the American people

Turning Points

WOODROW WILSON 1913-1921

Like Roosevelt before him, Woodrow Wilson regarded himself as the personal representative of the people. "No one but the President," he said, "seems to be expected ... to look out for the general interests of the country." He developed a program of progressive reform and asserted international leadership in building a New World Order. In 1917 he proclaimed American's entrance into World War I a crusade to make the world "safe for democracy."

Wilson had seen the frightfulness of war. He was born in Virginia in 1856, the son of a Presbyterian minister who during the Civil War was a pastor in Augusta, Georgia, and during Reconstruction a professor in the charred city of Columbia, South Carolina.

After graduation from Princeton (then the College of New Jersey) and the University of Virginia Law School, Wilson earned his doctorate at Johns Hopkins University and entered upon an academic career. In 1885 he married Ellen Louise Axson.

Wilson advanced rapidly as a conservative young professor of political science and became president of Princeton in 1902.

His growing national reputation led some conservative Democrats to consider him Presidential timber. First they persuaded him to run for Governor of New Jersey in 1910. In the campaign he asserted his independence of the conservatives and of the machine that had nominated him, endorsing a progressive platform, which he pursued as governor.

He was nominated for President at the 1912 Democratic Convention and campaigned on a program called the New Freedom, which stressed individualism and states' rights. In the three-way election he received only 42 percent of the popular vote but an overwhelming electoral vote.

Wilson maneuvered through Congress three major pieces of legislation. The first was a lower tariff, the Underwood Act; attached to the measure was a graduated Federal income tax. The passage of the Federal Reserve Act provided the Nation with the more elastic money supply it badly needed. In 1914 antitrust legislation established a Federal Trade Commission to prohibit unfair business practices.

Not mentioned in history that I have found.

In 1913, President Woodrow Wilson approved the Federal Reserve Act. A few years later, he reflected: "I am a most unhappy man. I have unwittingly ruined my country. A great industrial nation is controlled by its system of credit. Our system of credit is concentrated. The growth of the nation, therefore, and all our activities are in the hands of a few men...."

This one statement by Wilson also reflects the comments of Jefferson:

"If the American people ever allow private banks to control the issue of their currency, first by inflation, then by deflation, the banks. w i l l deprive the people of all property until their children wakeup homeless on the continent their fathers conquered. The issuing power should be taken from the banks and restored to the people, to whom it properly belongs." Thomas Jefferson

Another burst of legislation followed in 1916. One new law prohibited child labor; another limited railroad workers to an eight-hour day. By virtue of this legislation and the slogan "he kept us out of war," Wilson narrowly won re-election.

But after the election Wilson concluded that America could not remain neutral in the World War. On April 2, 1917, he asked Congress for a declaration of war on Germany.

Massive American effort slowly tipped the balance in favor of the Allies. Wilson went before Congress in January 1918, to enunciate American war aims the Fourteen Points, the last of which would establish "A general association of nations...affording mutual guarantees of political independence and territorial integrity to great and small states alike."

After the Germans signed the Armistice in November 1918, Wilson went to Paris to try to build an enduring peace. He later presented to the Senate the Versailles Treaty, containing the Covenant of the League of Nations, and asked, "Dare we reject it and break the heart of the world?"

But the election of 1918 had shifted the balance in Congress to the Republicans. By seven votes the Versailles Treaty failed in the Senate.

The President, against the warnings of his doctors, had made a national tour to mobilize public sentiment for the treaty. Exhausted, he suffered a stroke and nearly died. Tenderly nursed by his second wife, Edith Bolling Galt, he lived until 1924.

CALVIN COOLIDGE 1923-1929

At 2:30 on the morning of August 3, 1923, while visiting in Vermont, Calvin Coolidge received word that he was President. By the light of a kerosene lamp, his father, who was a notary public, administered the oath of office as Coolidge placed his hand on the family Bible.

Coolidge was "distinguished for character more than for heroic achievement," wrote a Democratic admirer, Alfred E. Smith. "His great task was to restore the dignity and prestige of the Presidency when it had reached the lowest ebb in our history... in a time of extravagance and waste "

Born in Plymouth, Vermont, on July 4, 1872, Coolidge was the son of a village storekeeper. He was graduated from Amherst College with honors, and entered law and politics in Northampton, Massachusetts. Slowly, methodically, he went up the political ladder from councilman in Northampton to Governor of Massachusetts, as a Republican. Enroute, he became thoroughly conservative.

As President, Coolidge demonstrated his determination to preserve the old moral and economic precepts amid the material prosperity which many Americans were enjoying. He refused to use Federal economic power to check the growing boom or to ameliorate the depressed condition of agriculture and certain industries. His first message to Congress in December 1923 called for isolation in foreign policy, and for tax cuts, economy, and limited aid to farmers.

He rapidly became popular. In 1924, as the beneficiary of what was becoming known as "Coolidge prosperity," he polled more than 54 percent of the popular vote.

In his Inaugural he asserted that the country had achieved "a state of contentment seldom before seen," and pledged himself to maintain the status quo. In subsequent years he twice vetoed farm relief bills, and killed a plan to produce cheap Federal electric power on the Tennessee River.

The political genius of President Coolidge, Walter Lippmann pointed out in 1926, was his talent for effectively doing nothing: "This active inactivity suits the mood and certain of the needs of the country admirably. It suits all the business interests which want to be let alone.... And it suits all those who have become convinced that government in this country has become dangerously complicated and top-heavy. "

Coolidge was both the most negative and remote of Presidents, and the most accessible. He once explained to Bernard Baruch why he often sat silently through interviews: "Well, Baruch, many times I say only 'yes' or 'no' to people. Even that is too much. It winds them up for twenty minutes more."

But no President was kinder in permitting him to be photographed in Indian war bonnets or cowboy dress, and in greeting a variety of delegations to the White House.

Both his dry Yankee wit and his frugality with words became legendary. His wife, Grace Goodhue Coolidge, recounted that a young woman sitting next to Coolidge at a dinner party confided to him she had bet she could get at least three words of conversation from him. Without looking at her he quietly retorted, "You lose." And in 1928, while vacationing in the Black Hills of South Dakota, he issued the most famous of his laconic statements, "I do not choose to run for President in 1928."

By the time the disaster of the Great Depression hit the country, Coolidge was in retirement. Before his death in January 1933, he confided to an old friend, " I feel I no longer fit in with these times."

Herbert Hoover – 31st President 1929-1933

Hoover was a son of Quaker blacksmith. He brought to the Presidency an unparalleled reputation for public service as an engineer, administrator, and humanitarian.

Born in an Iowa village in 1874, he grew up in Oregon. He enrolled at Stanford University when it opened in 1891, graduating as a mining engineer.

One week before Hoover celebrated his 40th birthday in London, Germany declared war on France, and the American Consul General asked his help in getting stranded tourists' home. In six weeks, his committee helped 120,000 Americans return to a far more difficult task, to feed Belgium, which had been overrun by the German army.

After the United States entered the war, President Wilson appointed Hoover head of the Food Administration. He succeeded in cutting consumption of foods needed overseas and avoided rationing at home, yet kept the Allies fed.

After the Armistice, Hoover, a member of the Supreme Economic Council and head of the American Relief Administration, organized shipments of food for starving millions in central Europe. He extended aid to famine-stricken Soviet Russia in 1921. When a critic inquired if he was not thus helping Bolshevism, Hoover retorted, "Twenty million people are starving. Whatever their politics, they shall be fed!"

Hoover served as Secretary of Commerce under Presidents Harding and Coolidge, Hoover became the Republican Presidential nominee in 1928. He said then: "We in America today are nearer to the final triumph over poverty than ever before in the history of any land." His election seemed to ensure prosperity. Within months the stock market crashed, and the Nation spiraled downward into depression.

After the crash Hoover announced that while he would keep the Federal Budget balanced, he would cut taxes and expand public works spending.
Cutting taxes was a good thing, but expanding public works was just the beginning. (The government starts down the path toward bigger government).

Sounds a lot like Obama and Company?

In 1931 repercussions from Europe deepened the crisis, even though the President presented to Congress a program asking for creation of the Reconstruction Finance Corporation to aid business, additional help for farmers facing mortgage foreclosure, banking reform, a loan to states for feeding the unemployed, expansion of public works, and drastic governmental economy.

At the same time, he reiterated his view that while people must not suffer from hunger and cold, caring for them must be primarily a local and voluntary responsibility.
His opponents in Congress, who felt were sabotaging his program for their own political gain, unfairly painted him as a callous and cruel President. Hoover became the scapegoat for the depression and was badly defeated in 1932. In the 1930's he became a powerful critic of the New Deal, warning against tendencies toward statisum.

Today, it is Socialism, President Obama, and this Congress.

Hoover trying to do the right thing was disarmed.

In 1947 President Truman appointed Hoover to a commission, which elected him chairman, to reorganize the Executive Departments. He was appointed chairman of a similar commission by President Eisenhower in 1953. Many economies resulted from both commissions' recommendations.

Franklin D. Roosevelt – 32nd President 1933-1945

Franklin came into the presidency during the depth of the Great Depression; he helped the American people regain faith in their selves. He brought hope as he promised prompt, vigorous action, and asserted in his Inaugural Address, "the only thing we have to fear is fear itself."

Today, President Obama, and this Congress are on the same page with Franklin.

Franklin started all kinds of government programs all of which are still to this day removing the rights of the people which are not in the Constitution. If Obama continues down this path with his extreme policies, this country will be lost forever.
The sad part with all that is going on is why this Congress is not doing anything! They are falling into the black hole and they have forgotten about their commitment to the People, their oath to the people and this country and the people they represent!

Franklin was elected to the office of President in 1932, to the first of four terms. By March there were 13,000,000 unemployed, and almost every bank was closed. In his first "hundred days," he proposed, and Congress enacted, a sweeping program to bring recovery to business and agriculture, relief to the unemployed and to those in danger of losing farms and homes, and reform, especially through the establishment of the Tennessee Valley Authority.

By 1935 the Nation had achieved some measure of recovery, but businessmen and bankers were turning more and more against Roosevelt's New Deal program. They feared his experiments, were appalled because he had taken the Nation off the gold standard and allowed deficits in the budget and disliked the concessions to labor. Franklin responded with a new program of reform: Social

Security, heavier taxes on the wealthy, new controls over banks and public utilities, and an enormous work relief program for the unemployed.

President Obama is seeking higher taxes on the wealthy and he has set a limit on what wealthy is: $250,000.00, control of the banks, cap and trade, control of car industry, more power to the Unions and most of all, spread the wealth.

Franklin had pledged the United States to the "good neighbor" policy, transforming the Monroe Doctrine from a Unilateral American manifesto into arrangements for mutual action against aggressors. He also sought through neutrality legislation to keep the United States out of the war in Europe, yet at the same time to strengthen nations threatened or attacked. When France fell and England came under siege in 1940', he began to send Great Britain all possible aid short of actual military involvement.

But there was another, with the Japanese attacking Pearl Harbor on December 7, 1941; Roosevelt directed organization of the Nation's manpower and resources for global war.

Roosevelt felt that the future peace of the world would depend upon relations between the United States and Russia, he devoted much thought to the planning of a United Nations, in which, he hoped, international difficulties could be settled.

By: White House Historical Association
      Washington, D.C.

"Unfortunately, the United Nations will never be the final hope for the countries on this globe. The only country that makes that call is the United States. We will be the ones to make the sacrifice for all nations large and small.

The United Nations is an organization without a ruder. They can pass resolution after resolution but have not means to control with force if needed, to make the resolution mean something. The only country that will is the United States.

However, if President Obama bankrupts the United States, the United States will not have the wherewithal to take action!

*At this time, we as a people are giving up our **Liberty!**"* Terry Bettis
5/29/09

There are many definitions of Liberty, I will give the 1828 version (Noah Webster and the 1970 version (Merriam Webster), you check out the current version!

LIBERTY – Noah Webster – 1828

1. Freedom from restraint, in a general sense, and applicable to the body, or to the will or mind. The body is at *liberty*, when not confined; the will or mind is at *liberty*, when not checked or controlled. A man enjoys *liberty*, when no physical force operates to restrain his actions or volitions.

2. *Natural liberty* consists in the power of acting as one thinks fit, without any restraint or control, except from the laws of nature. It is a state of exemption from the control of others, and from positive laws and the institutions of social life. This liberty is abridged by the establishment of government.

3. *Civil liberty* is the liberty of men in a state of society, or natural liberty, so far only abridged and restrained, as is necessary and expedient for the safety and interest of the society, state or nation. A restraint of natural liberty, not necessary or expedient for the public, is tyranny or oppression. Civil liberty is an exemption from the arbitrary will of others, which exemption is secured by established laws, which restrain every man from injuring or controlling another. Hence the restraints of law are essential to *civil liberty*.

> *The liberty of one depends not so much on the removal of all restraint from him, as on the due restraint upon the liberty of others.*
>
> *Ames.*
>
> *In this sentence, the latter word liberty denotes natural liberty.*

4. *Political liberty* is sometimes used as synonymous with civil liberty. But it more properly designates the *liberty of a nation*, the freedom of a nation or state from all unjust abridgment of its rights and

independence by another nation. Hence we often speak of the *political liberties* of Europe, or the nations of Europe.

5. *Religious liberty* is the free right of adopting and enjoying opinions on religious subjects, and of worshiping the Supreme Being according to the dictates of conscience, without external control.

I have given you 5 of the 10 meaning. I would encourage all that read this book to pull out their dictionary and check the current meaning of Liberty. It will surprise you more than you think. So much has changed over the decades with just this one word. This is the very reason our children think the way they do and why they do not have any understanding of our founding or the words that were spoken and the meaning thereof. I have to give you at least one example how the dictionary and the definitions have changed. It will be up to you to search more.

-Webster's Seventh New Collegiate

Dictionary- By: G. & C. Merriam CO. 1970

Definition of Liberty

The quality or state of being free; a: the power to do as one pleases b: freedom from physical restraint c: freedom from arbitrary or despotic control d: the positive enjoyment of various social, political, or economic right and privileges e: the power of choice

There are many more. When you compare, the definition has been lost and so has the meaning.

Chapter 6

The Price We Paid for Freedom

Liberty

Our nation's founding fathers knew how to count the cost of liberty

Turning Points

July 4, 1776, there was signed in the City of Philadelphia one of America's historic documents: the Declaration of Independence. It marked the birth of this nation which, **under God**, was destined for world leadership.

"With a firm reliance on the protection of Devine Providence, we mutually pledge to each other our lives, our fortunes, and our sacred honor."

"Would you make the same sacrifice today for your way of life and for your country?"

There were fifty-six (56) courageous men who signed that document understood that this was not just high-sounding rhetoric. They knew that if they succeeded, the best they could expect would be years of hardship in a struggling new nation. If they lost, they would face a hangman's noose as traitors to the British Crown.

The fifty-six (56), few were long to survive. Five were captured by the British and tortured before they died. Twelve had their homes, from Rhode Island to Charleston, sacked, looted, occupied by the enemy, or burned. Two lost their sons in the army. One had two sons captured. Nine of the fifty-six died in the war, from its hardships or from its bullets.

Whatever ideas you may have of the men who met that hot summer in Philadelphia, it is important that we remember certain facts about the men who made the pledge: they were not poor men, or pirates. They were men of means; rich men, most of them, who enjoyed the finer things of life. Not poor hungry men, but prosperous men, wealthy, secure in their prosperity, and respected in their communities.

They considered liberty more important than the security they enjoyed, and they pledged their lives, fortunes, and their honor. They fulfilled their pledge. Some among them paid the ultimate price. Freedom was won!

Someone has said, "To be born free is a privilege. To die free is an awesome responsibility."

Freedom is not free. It is always purchased at great cost.

John Adams did not know how significant his words would be when he spoke to his wife, Abigail, on passing the Declaration of Independence and said, "I am well aware of the toil, and blood, and treasure, that it will cost to maintain this declaration, and support and defend these states; yet, through all the gloom I can see the rays of light and glory. I can see the end is worth more than all the means."

To those who sacrificed for our freedom, the end was worth the painful means:

"Posterity-you will never know how much it has cost my generation to preserve your freedom. I hope you will make good use of it."
John Quincy Adams

"What we obtain too cheaply, we esteem too lightly; it is dearness only that gives everything its value.

Heaven knows how to put a price upon its goods and it would be strange indeed if so celestial an article as freedom should not be highly rated."
Thomas Payne, 1776

"For the support of this declaration, with a firm reliance on the protection of the Divine Providence, we mutually pledge to each other, our lives, our fortunes, and our sacred honor." Declaration of Independence.

Chapter 7

Why America is great?

Turning Points

The abundance of America is unprecedented in history; and freedoms which are the envy of the world?

Most of the world peoples go to bed at night hungry. The rest are under control of Communist rule, Socialists domination, religious Emmons of the Muslim faith, where freedom, as Americans know it, simply does not exist.

Is President Obama a traitor to this nation? Is he bought and paid for by socialist Americans, Islamic fascist, and the global socialist elite. No immigration should be allowed if the religious creed of those whom wish to come here is Jihad. No Muslims should be allowed to immigrate; their faith precludes being good Americans upholding freedom and liberty.

Is the abundance and this freedom by chance? Americans like to perceive that is their right!

Is it?

For the American people, our rights lay in the Bible, the Constitution and the Bill of Rights and our Republic!

"If God indeed has blessed America, why"?

The best of America was stated by one of our most moving patriotic hymns that cites the beauty of America. When Katherine Lee Bates stood atop Pike's Peak and scanned the sweep of the land, and she wrote the "Purple Mountain Majesties," and "Amber Waves of Grain." She said: "God had shed His Grace on this land". – A vast unexplored wilderness that, in an astonishingly short period, grew into a great nation.

America has been blessed with an abundance of natural resources, oil, natural gas, uranium, coal ore, timber, water, soil and the climate to grow all things. Combine these elements and we have the perfect climate to nourish a civilization the ability to shine from sea to shining sea.

Lynam Abbott once said: *"A nation is made great, not by its fruitful acres, but by the men who cultivate them: not by its great forests, but by the men who use them; not by its mines, but by the men who build and run them. America was a great land when Columbus discovered it: Americans have made of it a great nation."*

The American Spirit pioneered this continent, subdued the elements that worked against them and encouraged people from all over the world the dream of coming to this great land. The American initiative and ingenuity are known across the world. The government was not involved in the lives of the everyday American like it is today. Then, other nations looked on America in awe, at her ability over the decades to produce more than her needs, but enough to feed the masses and meet the needs for many more. (God taught us how to grow in abundance!) God knew the demands that would eventually be called upon the American people.

The Free Enterprise system and the spirit of the American people without government interference gave the American people the ability to produce more goods and services at a lower cost. This economic genius made it possible to produce millions of jobs – in factories, on the farm and in the professions of many others. This gave the American people the income to buy the goods they produced and allowed the excess to be export to the world. This philosophy was the beginning of a Nation that would become so generous to the rest of the world that today is looked upon as an obligation to feed the world.

For the most part the American people have never had to escape the specter of wide scale hunger on her on soil. We have been blessed. We had the great depression which caused the food lines; we had the dust bowl in the farm lands that ruined the crops. But, for most, they were prepared for such a catastrophe. Today, they are dependent on the grocery store; they do not have a food source or storage in the event of an event that could alter their lives for months and maybe years!

However, even in the most trying times, the American people managed to give what little they had to help their neighbors, friends and in some cases others across the sea.

America has always been a country that will give to others outside her lands. She has given generously to every nation, and sometimes her own enemies, in time of emergency. She has given to all in spite of the government. The government cannot give what it does not have; only the American people can do that!

This government has passed more social legislation and enacted more laws providing individual liberty than any other nation in the world. She has given the American people the "Bill of Rights" which gave them the right of freedom of speech, the right to bare arms and many other rights. With these rights, she has been able to open her cause to the world and those other dictatorships that control their people, the press, etc., look on amazed and defeated. So, they became more controlling of their people, less freedoms and more government control.

Today, she is taking more control of the people, its ability to produce goods and services and dictating how the American people will be controlled.

All of these blessings that we had, point back to her foundations and to the providential hand of God. The purple mountain majesties and the fruited plains originated with God. American's blessing call for thanksgiving from all those who enjoy them. The spiritual heritage that built America unfolded by design. (God's Will.) God in his divine intervention and the Founders belief in God; gave the founders the ability to create the American democracy, the U.S. Constitution, the Bill of Rights and the great freedoms they ensure.

This country was put on this earth for a reason. It is obvious to a person who truly understands the saga of events that shaped this country. We will not only take a look back but we as a people need to understand better what is happening today and where America stands in the world, how she arrived and where she is headed during these trying times.

"Can the liberties of a nation be secure, when we have removed the conviction that these liberties are the gift of God?" Thomas Jefferson

I can only say what Thomas Jefferson said:

"My God! How little do my countrymen know what precious blessings they are in possession of, and which no other people on earth enjoy?"

Chapter 8

Setting the Foundation Without Government intervention

Turning Points

Americans need to take a look back, back to their beginning, back to 1620 at Plymouth Rock.

When Americans look back to their beginning, they will always go back to a small band of people that landed in 1620 at Plymouth Rock. There were more than a hundred Pilgrims aboard the Mayflower, and most of them were Christians. There were also separatists who wanted to change the Church of England and build a new life in an unknown wilderness, where they could worship the Lord in the way they believed the Scriptures taught.

The Pilgrims wanted their own Law and Order when they came to the new Land.

They committed themselves to the will of God and resolved to proceed. The ship finally came within sight of Cape Cod on November 19, 1620. They scanned the shoreline just to the west of them and described it as a godly land with lots of forests on the brink of the ocean. Which was true of Cape Cod at the time? They had no sanction they were going ashore at Cape Cod at this time. "This was no man's land." So they moved out into deep waters again while everyone aboard pondered what to do. Their decision, the Mayflower Compact, would be the deciding factor!

Originally intended as a temporary pact to keep the law and order among themselves in a wilderness with no law and order, yet that historic agreement laid the foundations of law and order and established the first

"Civil body politic in America."

The pilgrims new that the Compact must lie in their heart, they knew that the conviction of God must be at the center of all law and order and law without a moral base will be no law at all.

They also knew that the compact would rest on the "Covenant" and agreement that would later help lay the foundation of the American Republic. All laws would rest **not** upon a monarchy or a dictatorship, but upon _"the consent of the governed."_ I talked about this in my first book "Guards at the Gate". This is the reason the inscription at the Plymouth Rock monument says:

"They laid the foundation of a state wherein every man through countless ages should have Liberty."

When they signed the *Mayflower Compact*, according to William Bradford, "They came to the harbor…Compassed, being glad they were leaving the sea. They could see the pine trees and others and smell the fragrance therein." Years later, they "Blessed the God of heaven, who had brought them over the ocean and a sea of trouble." 'Let them, therefore, praise the Lord, for he is good and His mercies endure forever.' (Quoted from the Geneva Bible: used by the Pilgrims.)"

"Lastly, our ancestors established their system of government on morality and religious sentiment. Moral habits, they believed, cannot safely be trusted on any other foundation than religious principle, nor any government is secure which is not supported by moral habits."

Daniel Webster

Chapter 9

Christian Heritage

Our Nation was founded on a commitment to God and the Principles of His Word.

Turning Points

In 1787, representatives met in Philadelphia to write the Constitution of the United States, "(A document long forgotten by all of our current leaders and never understood by most, the Constitution.)" Terry Bettis 5/27/09
Benjamin Franklin @ age 81 in Philadelphia.

"In the beginning of the contest with Britain, when we were sensible of danger, we had daily prayers in this room for Divine protection. Our prayers, Sir, were heard and they were graciously answered. All of us who were engaged in the struggle must have observed frequent instances of a superintending Providence in our favor...Have we now forgotten this powerful Friend? Or do we imagine we no longer need His assistance?"

"I have lived, Sir, a long time, and the longer I live, the more convincing proofs I see of this truth: that God governs in the affairs of man. And if a sparrow cannot fall to the ground without His notice, is it probable that an empire can rise without His aid? We have been assured, Sir, in the Sacred Writings that except the Lord build the house, they labor in vain that build it. I firmly believe this...

"I therefore beg leave to move that, henceforth, prayers imploring the assistance of Heaven and its blessing on our deliberation be held in this assembly every morning."

The purpose of the pilgrims in 1620 was to establish a government based on the Bible. The New England Charter, signed by King James I, confirmed this goal. Advance the Christian religion, to the glory of God.

Bradford, in his writing of the Pilgrims landing described their first act: "being thus arrived in a good harbor and brought safe to land, they fell upon their knees and blessed the God of heaven..."

Rhode Island Charter of 1683 begins: "We submit our persons, lives, and estates unto our Lord Jesus Christ, the King of kings and Lord of lords and all those perfect and most absolute laws of His given us in His Holy Word." Those "absolute laws" became the basis of our Declaration of Independence, which includes in its first paragraph an appeal to the laws of nature and of nature's God. Our national Constitution established a republic upon the "absolute laws" of the Bible, not a democracy based on the changing whims of people.

In his inaugural address to Congress, the First president of our nation "George Washington" stressed God's role in the birth of this republic:

"No people can be bound to acknowledge and adore the invisible hand which conducts the affairs of men more than the people of the United States. Every step by which they have advanced to the character of an independent nation seems to have been distinguished by some token of providential agency. We ought to be no less persuaded that the propitious smiles of heaven cannot be expected on a nation that disregards the eternal rules of order and right, which heaven itself has ordained."

This continued through the decades of history, one will find in the inaugural addresses of all the Presidents, and in the Constitution of all fifty of our states, without exception, references to the Almighty God of the universe, the Author and Sustainer of our liberty.

Throughout our history, our forefathers have given eloquent testimony of our commitment to God and His Principles:

"It is the duty of nations, as well as of men, to own their dependence upon the overruling power of God and to recognize the sublime truth announced in the Holy Scripture and proven by all history, that those nations only are blessed whose God is the Lord." Abraham Lincoln

"The religion which has introduced civil liberty is the religion of Christ and His Apostles...to this we owe our free constitutions of government." Noah Webster

The very final word of our National Anthem puts it into context:

"Blessed with victory and peace, may this Heav'n-rescued land Praise the Power that hath made and preserved us a nation! Then conquer we must, when our cause it is just; and this is our motto: 'In God is our trust!' And the Star - Spangled Banner in triumph shall wave o'er the land of the free, and the home of the brave."

Today, we have *President Obama*, saying on foreign soil that we are not a Christian Nation based on Christian Principles. Did I miss something in our History?

"Man is just a very small part of God's plan for this great Nation. God has determined that this Nation will do the necessary acts to ensure the freedoms of the American people and to preserve other Nations in the process. It will never be up to Man." Terry W. Bettis 5/27/2009

"The moral principles and precepts contained in the Scriptures ought to form the basis of all our civil constitutions and laws. All the miseries and evils which men suffer from vice, crime, ambition, injustice, oppression, slavery, and war, proceed from their despising or neglecting the precepts contained in the Bible."

NOAH WEBSTER

"The first and almost the only Book deserving of universal attention is the Bible."

JOHN QUINCY ADAMS

"All the good from the Savior of the world is communicated through this Book; but for the Book we could not know right from wrong. All the things desirable to man are contained in it."

ABRAHAM LINCOLN

"...the Bible...is the one supreme source of revelation of the meaning of life, the nature of God and Spiritual nature and need of men. It is the only guide of life which really leads the spirit in the way of peace and salvation."

WOODROW WILSON

"Go to the Scriptures...the joyful promises it contains will be a balsam to all your troubles."

ANDREW JACKSON

"The foundations of our society and our government rest so much on the teachings of the Bible that it would be difficult to support them if faith in these teachings would cease to be practically universal in our country."

CALVIN COOLIDGE

Chapter 10

Breakdown of the Family Structure Declining morality is destroying our nation's Families

Turning Points

"We have all seen the statistics that reveal the breakdown of the family unit in our society…more than one out of every two couples who walk down the aisle to get married will eventually change their minds and end up in a divorce court; last year over 600,000 children were born to unmarried women; each month the life of 125,000 children are cruelly ended before they were given a chance to leave their mother's womb; an estimated 10 million Americans are engaged in perverse, homosexual relationships. The tragedy is that these statistics represent human lives…real people who are experiencing the consequences of refusal to follow God's plan for the family." Del Fehsenfeld

For years the family unit has been disintegrating and will not survive this century unless we change the mind thoughts of our young! After all, they are the ones that will have to deal with this problem. One might want to read the following books to get a better understanding: *The Death of the Family*, by a British physician suggests doing away with the family because it is a primary conditioning device for a Western, imperialistic world view, or *Sexual Politics*, by Kate Millett. She writes that the family must go because it oppresses and enslaves women.

Is this country in danger that the American family will cease to exist? I hope not. More Americans marry, have children, and commit themselves to a family life and a family unit. However, we do have concerns, not that the family unit will disappear, but that certain trends relevant to today will decapitate the family, destroy its integrity, and cause its members to suffer such crippling emotional conflicts that they will become a burden to society.

The family unit is being destroyed by the right to marry same sex unions. This will eventually destroy marriage as we know it. We have states that are trying to pass laws that will allow it. If we continue to go down this path, then the act of marriage will have no meaning between one man and one woman.

God, that's right, God, determined that long before any of us were given this right to be born. Check out the book of Genesis in the Bible, the same Bible that was used to determine the foundation of this country. God knew and our Founders knew that we would have to face these challenges and He gave us the tools to defend it. However, the leaders over the years forgot or never knew the meaning, and in their steed, they did not want to spend the time to research or did not care, to research our history. So, are we slowly going down the drain, flushed into the sewer of history and forever lost in our beliefs? (Remember Rome!).

Every animal on this earth knows how to appropriate. They know that they seek the opposite sex, not the same sex. The same sex is not compatible to reproduce. Even though God gave us the ability to think and create great things in this country, He did not intend for us to destroy our values and morals. The Liberal thinking of this country will destroy this country in the end. Their agenda (Liberal) believes that everything is ok and when there is a problem the Liberal Government will raise more taxes to fix it. Eventually, there will be no one to pay the taxes to adhere to this insanity, and the United States as we know it will fall and the American Dream will be lost forever. The World and all of its countries will no longer have a country of such bounty and promise to come too. The opportunity for all will be lost in the mist of what could have been. We will no longer be the country of plenty and opportunity!

Is this what you want for your children and your Country?

I want to talk about the divorce rate in this country, but I will say that commitment to each other during good and bad times are up to the couple that made the commitment to say the vows. It has become too easy to flush the marriage and forget about the kids, then move on down the road to another that will end in the same.

More and more women are moving into the work force outside the home and less and less staying home to tend to the children and the family unit. What happens is: they become more involved in corporate life, influences and forget about the family unit. This is not the problem for women; it is the problem of this government. This government has created a foundation that in order to survive both parents must work and the government schools will take control of teaching the children.

"Another Turning Point"?

And so, the government took control of the family and their children. Check the books in schools and the teaching they provide. No wonder more and more parents that understand, are home schooling their children. It is sad that we gave this government so much control over our lives. The worst part is that our children will have to pay for our discretions!

"Parents today often resent Children because they interfere with Their Fulfillment."

Our Nation today appears confused morally more than any time in her history. We need to hear less about self-fulfillment and more about self-denial. Is denial the key to fulfillment?

We need to hear more about the worth of a human being, not abortion. That one child transcends time and significance over all other secular views put together.

It is time for all of us to take the time to look at vertical relationships, and for that relationship to transcend to family members, at home or away. Even though, knowing they need us as much as we need them.

Today we are seeing an all-out assault on the family in America. It is coming from all directions. Our only defense is in the Word!

We will have to build a wall of defense and protection around the family unit and use the family as a strong base to turn our nation back to God.

But, we still have idiots out there who do not care about the family unit. One such idiot is:

David Letterman is in the hot seat for several crude jokes he made on CBS' "The Late Show" about Sarah Palin and her 14-year-old teenage daughter.

Letterman, in his monologue Monday night, noted that the 2008 Republican vice-presidential candidate attended a Yankees game during a trip to New York City, where she was honored by a special needs group. Letterman referred to Palin, Alaska's governor, as having the style of a "slutty flight attendant."

The "Late Show" host also took a shot at Palin's daughter, while poking fun at the Yankees' third baseman.

"One awkward moment for Sarah Palin at the Yankee game," Letterman said, "during the seventh inning, her daughter was knocked up by Alex Rodriguez."

The backlash was almost immediate, with Palin's supporters denouncing the CBS host for making jokes that many said were sexist and for what they called an unfair attack on the governor and her family.

"I think that calling the former vice presidential candidate a slut or saying that her daughter was knocked up by Alex Rodriguez, I think everyone can agree that's over the line," Washington Examiner correspondent Byron York told FOX News' Greta Von Susteren.

But an even more disturbing fact, which Letterman may not have known, was that the daughter who accompanied Palin on her trip to New York was 14-year-old Willow not 18-year-old Bristol, the unwed mother of Palin's first grandchild.

Now, many critics   including the Palin's themselves – are slamming Letterman for jokes that they say make light of sexual abuse of an underage girl.

In a statement to FOXNews.com, Palin accused Letterman of making "sexually perverted" and "inappropriate" comments that she doubted he would "ever dare make" about anyone else's daughter.

"Acceptance of inappropriate sexual comments about an underage girl, who could be anyone's daughter, contributes to the atrociously high rate of sexual exploitation of minors by older men who use and abuse others," she said.

Palin's husband, Todd, echoed her sentiments, telling FOXNews.com, "Any 'jokes' about raping my 14-year-old are despicable. Alaskans know it, and I believe the rest of the world knows it, too."

A representative for "The Late Show" declined to offer comment for this story.

This is just one example of the hypocrisy of the news media! They feel that one word just boils my blood (The Liberals are all about how they feel and if it feels right to them than that is OK) (This is bull shit) (I do not want to know you're feeling), anything that has to do with the family unit, and sure mistakes are made during one's life but will it be on such a destructive mode?

Just because you do not like ones views does not give you the right to try to destroy anyone and any family.

Fire the Bastard! I have had enough of this type of destruction, have you?

When you go back and research history if you believe in the family and the values of the family, I hope you will be appalled by this blatant attack on this one family. **_What if this were your family?_**

"This entire comment from David Letterman means to me, that he does not care about the family; the family is fare game in the political world and the comic world. He should be fired immediately! To him it is a game. As far as I am concerned his game is over! Flush him down the sewer and the station (CBS) that broadcast such garbage! Pull their license, shut them down and pull out all the idiots that are running CBS. They are nothing but wimps. I bet you could not find one there that has the balls to stand up for Sara or her family."

⸻

"The family has always been the cornerstone of American society. Our families nurture, preserve and pass on to each succeeding generation the values we share and cherish, values that are the foundation for our freedoms. In the family, we learn our first lessons of God and man, love and discipline, rights and responsibilities, human dignity and human frailty.

Our families give us daily examples of these lessons being put into practice. In raising and instructing our children, in providing personal and compassionate care for the elderly, in maintaining the spiritual strength of religious commitment among our people in these and other ways, America's families make immeasurable contributions to America's well being.

Today more than ever, it is essential that these contributions be not taken for granted and that each of us remembers that the strength of our families is vital to the strength of our nation."
– Ronald Reagan -

"Modern western humanistic teaching places total emphasis on the individual's selfish desires; social responsibility no longer being anything of concern. Added to this is the liberal view that religion is irrelevant; one is as good as another; the feeble minded still believe in a supreme being rather than accept the "fact" of evolution. We are reaping the results of these misguided world views. I'm not convinced anything is too late. But clearly unabated immigration and low birth rates have consequences."

- Toby Passaro Bel Air. Texas –

"Makes one wonder why this Christian Nation has let 50,000,000+ babies be destroyed since Roe v Wade January 1973. Our children are the life blood of this country. If we do not encourage our youth to reproduce more and more, than we as a Christian Nation will go down. America will cease to exist, it is also another reason that immigration has to stop both legal and illegal. We have to get our country back."

Terry Bettis 6/1/2009

These kinds of problems are designed not to crush us, but to crowd us toward Jesus Christ, Who provided the remedy for sin by shedding His blood on the cross.

The problem of sin is real and terrible, but it brings with it the possibility that we can be forgiven and draped in the righteousness of Christ. Only in Him can we rebuild the walls that sin has destroyed.

As stated by: Adrian Rogers (The Problem of Family Breakdown)

He stated: "I want to consider another wall that is broken down today. Dear Friend, the walls of the home have fallen in on the family! Indeed, the home is rapidly becoming a domestic disaster area.

We're talking about the need to visualize a problem before you can turn it into a possibility. But the fact is that when it comes to the home, you don't have to picture the problem. It's all around us! If your neighborhood is typical, there are broken homes right on your street. The walls of our homes have fallen." When it comes to marriage:

"People need to quit jumping into marriage so quickly and taking it lightly. I'm not judging just giving advice as someone who has been there. Let me put it this way. Being married to the right man is like going commando. It's free, exhilarating, you can feel your blood running through your veins. Being married to the wrong man is like being a thong. You're stuck in the butt crack of life staring at an asshole all day!" by Erin Norvell, Eunice, NM

Chapter 11

Education in America Another Turning Point
What did we do?

Turning Points

What is government? When this question is asked, most people respond by equating government solely with a centralized state. Even our language reflects the confusion: "Government? It's in Washington," or "The government will take care of its citizens through its many programs." Both of these statements reflect a misunderstanding of the true nature of government. They portray the idea that the only governing institution is a political one. Historically, however, the term "government" was always qualified in some way, unlike our present-day definitions.

Our educational system reflects the same confusion. A generation ago or more our high school classes dealing with state government were given the title "Civics." The emphasis was on the function of government in civil matters. Today, that is no longer the case. Such classes are now given the broad title of "Government," implying that the many governments are absorbed into one all- encompassing government.

Before World War I, textbooks dealing with national government were qualified with the title "Civil." An example of such books can be found in 1903: *Elements of Civil Government. According to its author,* "The Family...is a form of government, established for the good of children themselves, and the first government that each of us must obey" The book continues by defining five areas of civil government:

"The Township or civil district, the village or the city, the county, the State,

Those that wrote the textbooks were also aware that there were personal, family, church, school and civil governments, each having a legitimate realm of authority. The state was seen as only one government among many.

Noah Webster stated:

"The moral principles and precepts contained in the scriptures ought to form the basis of all our civil constitutions and laws. All the miseries and evils which men suffer from vice, crime, ambition, injustice, oppression, slavery, and war, proceed from their despising or neglecting the precepts contained in the Bible."

"The basic government is self-government, and only the Christian man is truly free and hence able properly to exercise self-government. A free social order rests on the premise that self-government is the basic government in the human order, and that any weakening of or decline in self-government means a decline in responsibility and the rise of tyranny and slavery" (R.J. Rushdoony, Politics of Guilt and Pity, p. 3).

"There are few statements today about the opportunity and the obligation of a Christian home in a Republic. Yet there is no single element in America which contributes more significantly to the success of Christian Constitutional government. It is in the home where the foundations of Christian character are laid. It is in the home where Christian self-government is learned and practiced. Yet, the Christian American who is aware of the particular challenges to America's Christian character and to the Constitutional form of government still inclines to political education outside the home. Thus, while parents are active politically, educationally, religiously, it becomes necessary for other agencies   the school, the church, the community   to pick up the responsibility for making home the first sphere of government in the republic. Needless to say they cannot substitute what only the home can provide" (Rosalie J. Slater, Teaching and Learning America's Christian History, p. 3).

As stated by: Adrian Rogers (The Problem of Education)

"Another problem is that our educational system has taken God, His Word, prayers and put them outside the walls of our schools. They are no longer welcome.

With God on the outside, what is now on the inside, Evolution, homosexuality, and illicit sex? Abortion and venereal disease are in, too. But God is out.

The concept of absolute truth is also outside the walls of our schools for the most part. The baby-boomer generation has drunk deeply at the poison springs of relativism, and the children of this generation exhibit that Malay. The idea that there is absolute right and wrong is viewed as a curiosity, a throwback to a more primitive generation.

All of this leads to an inevitable result: the walls of education are broken down. Psalm 11:3 says: "If the foundation be destroyed, what can the righteous do?" We sing "God Bless America," but why should He bless us unless we repent?

Some say, "Pastor, why are you drawing such a grim picture?" Because we must see the problem in all of its ugliness before we can see God's possibilities in it."

Take Notes:

_____

_____

_____

_____

_____

_____

_____

_____

_____

_____

_____

_____

_____

_____

_____

_____

_____

_____

_____

_____

_____

_____

_____

Chapter 12

The Schools and the Progressives

Turning Points

There were many crusades during the 1830's and 1840's none accomplished as much as did the reforms in education. The idea of public schools took root in Massachusetts. In 1647 the colony passed a law that every town of fifty householders must hire a person to teach reading and writing to the children who came and asked to learn.

Nearly two hundred years later Massachusetts took the lead once again when Horace Mann, a young Bostonian lawyer, was appointed secretary of the first State Board of Education. Although Massachusetts had passed a law establishing public high schools ten years before Horace Mann was appointed, there were only about a dozen in the entire state. Yet, Massachusetts had more than any other state. Addressing a group of honor students at Harvard University in 1850, a speaker made this remark:

"If there be any single trait by which the historian will distinguish the present from all past ages, it is the rage for reform. It agitates every nation and all classes; and it comprehends nearly every subject of thought and action. Everywhere on every matter, and in all ways, the great heart of humanity throbs for reform."

Class distinctions had little chance to rise on a fast-moving frontier where rich and poor shared alike in the struggle for food, shelter, and comforts in an undeveloped country.

Education grew as the country grew.

Education has been considered important since colonial days. In 1636, just sixteen years after the landing of the Pilgrims, Harvard College was established in the British Colonies.

Religion, morality, and knowledge being necessary to good government and the happiness of mankind, schools and the means of education shall forever be encouraged.

In the early days, schooling for children was provided by parents in the home, church, and private schools. Children on the large southern plantations had tutors who lived with the families. Not until a little over thirty years after the end of the War for Independence was the first system of schools started for every child at public expense. The reforms of the 1840's improved the public schools.

There is more history that I could dwell into but at a later date.

In 1867, the National Bureau of Education was formed, but later in 1979 the department of education, which is a Cabinet level department of the United States government. Created by the Department of Education Organization Act (Public Law 96-88), it was signed into law by President Jimmy Carter on October 17, 1979 and began operating on May 16, 1980.

The social progressives knew in order to get their agenda moving forward they needed to get into the minds of the children. The parents and grandparents were from the old school and their mind set was already set in stone. The progressives moved quickly to infiltrate the schools and the textbooks. The history of the United States was altered in the textbooks one chapter at a time. Instead of American history, it was a history that would not offend non-white Americans. Not understanding that the history was about all Americans, their struggles and contributions to America. The progressives knew exactly what they wanted and intended to get it.

Since the late 70's, the schools have been transformed into social teaching machines for the Progressives.

"The biggest problem with America today is that middle school, high school pupils and even college students have gotten increasingly more stupid over the years because the enemies down the street now control our schools and teach our children. But instead of teaching them the honest facts of history and science that you and I were taught in the 1940s, 1950s and early 1960s the **Rockefeller Foundation, the Rockefeller Brothers Foundation, the Pew Foundation, the Ford Foundation,** *and the* **Carnegie Trust** *took control of the NEA and the curriculum. Instead of learning about the Constitution and the Declaration of Independence, our children are taught about the UN Charter and the UN Covenant on Human Rights. Instead of being taught American history, students are taught world history. Instead of being taught social sciences, students are taught about social justice. And, instead of being taught family values, students are taught they have social equality with their parents under the law with rights that include suing their parents. Their instructors teach them that, regardless of what their parents think, they have the right to be sexually active regardless of the moral values or religious upbringing of their families. In fact, the school will provide both middle school and high school boys and girls with condoms so they can practice safe sex without the fear of becoming pregnant.*

Once sex education became part of the curriculum of Winston Elementary School in southeast Washington, DC it quickly became a "hands-on" activity. On Monday, April 7, 1997 four girls and five boys, ages 9 years to 12, disrobed in an empty detention room and, for 30 minutes with the lights off and the door locked, engaged in oral sex. According to a report in the Washington Times on April 14, 1997 (pg. A1) the school principle **Ronald Parker** *learned about the sexual tryst shortly after it happened but he failed to notify neither the police nor any of the parents of the students involved. Most of the parents learned about the incident on Friday, April 18 when those involved began bragging about it to other students. The parents of the girls involved wanted to the boys charged with rape.* **Parker,** *who told the Washington Times he never reported the incident because, in his words, "...the sex was consensual," didn't believe any crime was committed. In other words, the social progressives the enemy down the street actually believe it does take a village to raise a child, and that village has* *a right to determine the moral norms for your children regardless how you feel about it.*

And what did Hillary Clinton say regarding a village?

*To the social progressive, as long as the child involved is not their child, a 9-year old girl can consent to have sex even though she isn't legally old enough to decide whether or not she can stay up past her regular bedtime. A week after the Winston Elementary incident, on April 16, 1997 at the August Martin High School in Queens, New York, four teenage boys lured a 14-year-old girl into an unused classroom and raped her. Three of the boys, **DeShawn James,** 17; **Valijean Lee**, 18; and **Vincent Dowdy**, 17 "allegedly" gang-raped the girl while she was restrained by the fourth boy, **Charles Baskerville,** 18. Police investigators said that minutes before the attack two of the boys went to the guidance counselor's office and asked for condoms so they could have safe sex. I doubt they told the guidance counselor they were holding a 14-year old hostage in one of the classrooms so they could rape her. On May 20, a 17-year old junior girl was sexually assaulted by four boys at the same school 38 days after the first incident. (The New York Times; May 21, 1997, Metro Section.)*

Every social progressive society in modern times has been quick to realize the key to the future stability of the socialist political system it fostered was in the psychological exploitation of its children. The manipulation of the minds to rid children of their home grown moral values begins with desensitization to eradicate what the national education system calls the "ignorance of the religious right," either with elaborate exercises on evolution to prove that man was not created by God; or by inducing the children to accept deviant lifestyles as normal alternatives to heterosexuality and in many cases, both. Social progressive teachers believe it is their responsibility to reshape the minds of their students and correct the errors taught to them by their parents particularly those which deal with patriotic issues or theological matters. In the mind of the social progressive, you do not have the right to worship as you please if your theological views offend anyone else. Unless, of course, if you are Muslim... And, if you are a Christian and have been taught to view homosexuality as a sin, the social progressive and the society they now influence through the liberal media will view you as a racist.

It is this dichotomy that has led to the societal mess America now faces. With the best public school system in the world, the United States has roughly 28 million functional illiterates and approximately 83 million people who are classified as "learning impaired." Who's to blame? Ultimately the princes of industry and the barons of business and banking are deliberately financing the dummying down of America to make sure the working class of America doesn't understand what's happening to their country. But, while the agenda is set from "on high," you still have to blame the social progressive in the classrooms who take their marching orders from the social progressives who head the socialist school districts.

The dummying down of America is important to the social progressives because the money barons know if you're too dumb to understand what rights you possess, you won't know when you lose them. Talk to the average yokel on the street and ask him where his rights come from, and nine-times-out-of-ten, they will tell you their rights come from the laws enacted by Congress; or at least, from the government. Most young people don't realize that rights come from God, and those rights were hammered into the Constitution of the United States in places like Lexington, Concord or Valley Forge and reinforced by the Bill of Rights. Since the start of the politicization of the federal courts in 1935, Congress has done everything it can to circumvent the Constitution by appointing social progressives, regardless of their judicial qualifications, as federal judges." - Jon Ryter

The Progressives are very patient in their efforts but once an opening is created, they will jump on it with a vengeance, knowing full well that they have a limited amount of time to do their deed before the people wake up.

With each opening they take and get, it is another notch in the handle of their gun and one more sword in the Constitution of the United States and the Bill of Rights.

Chapter 13

The Monetary Breakdown of the West

Turning Points

To understand the current monetary chaos, it is necessary to trace briefly the international monetary developments of the 20th century, and to see how each set of unsound inflationist interventions has collapsed of its own inherent problems, only to set the stage for another round of interventions. The 20th- century history of the world monetary order can be divided into nine phases. Let us examine each in turn.

Phase I: The Classical Gold Standard, 1815–1914

We can look back upon the "classical" gold standard, the Western world of the 19th and early 20th centuries, as the literal and metaphorical Golden Age. With the exception of the troublesome problem of silver, the world was on a gold standard, which meant that each national currency (the dollar, pound, franc, etc.) was merely a name for a certain definite weight of gold. The "dollar," for example, was defined as 1/20 of a gold ounce, the pound sterling as slightly less than 1/4 of a gold ounce, and so on. This meant that the "exchange rates" between the various national currencies were fixed, not because they were arbitrarily controlled by government, but in the same way that one pound of weight is defined as being equal to sixteen ounces.

The international gold standard meant that the benefits of having one money medium were extended throughout the world. One of the reasons for the growth and prosperity of the United States has been the fact that we have enjoyed one money. Throughout the large area of the country, we have had gold or at least a single dollar standard within the entire country, and did not have to suffer the chaos of each city and county issuing its own money, which would then fluctuate with respect to the moneys of all the other cities and counties. The 19th century saw the benefits of one money throughout the civilized world. One money facilitated freedom of trade, investment, and travel throughout that trading and monetary area, with the consequent growth of specialization and the international division of labor.

It must be emphasized that gold was not selected arbitrarily by governments to be the monetary standard. Gold had developed for many centuries on the free market as the best money; as the commodity providing the most stable and desirable monetary medium. Above all, the supply and provision of gold was subject only to market forces, and not to the arbitrary printing press of the government.

The international gold standard provided an automatic market mechanism for checking the inflationary potential of government. It also provided an automatic mechanism for keeping the balance of payments of each country in equilibrium. As the philosopher and economist David Hume pointed out in the mid-18th century, if one nation, say France, inflates its supply of paper francs, its prices rise; the increasing incomes in paper francs stimulate imports from abroad, which are also spurred by the fact that prices of imports are now relatively cheaper than prices at home.

At the same time, the higher prices at home discourage exports abroad; the result is a deficit in the balance of payments, which must be paid for by foreign countries cashing in francs for gold. The gold outflow means that France must eventually contract its inflated paper francs in order to prevent a loss of all of its gold. If the inflation has taken the form of bank deposits, then the French banks have to contract their loans and deposits in order to avoid bankruptcy as foreigners call upon the French banks to redeem their deposits in gold. The contraction lowers prices at home, and generates an export surplus, thereby reversing the gold outflow until the price levels are equalized in France and in other countries as well.

It is true that the interventions of governments previous to the 19th century weakened the speed of this market mechanism and allowed for a business cycle of inflation and recession within this gold-standard framework. These interventions were particularly: the governments' monopolizing of the mint, legal tender laws, the creation of paper money, and the development of inflationary banking propelled by each of the governments. But while these interventions slowed the adjustments of the market, these adjustments were still in ultimate control of the situation. So while the classical gold standard of the 19th century was not perfect, and allowed for relatively minor booms and busts, it still provided us with by far the best monetary order the world has ever known, an order which worked, which kept business cycles from getting out of hand, and which enabled the development of free international trade, exchange, and investment.

Phase II: World War I and After

If the classical gold standard worked so well, why did it break down? It broke down because governments were entrusted with the task of keeping their monetary promises, of seeing to it that pounds, dollars, francs, etc., were always redeemable in gold as they and their controlled banking system had pledged. It was not gold that failed; it was the folly of trusting government to keep its promises. To wage the catastrophic war of World War I, each government had to inflate its own supply of paper and bank currency. So severe was this inflation that it was impossible for the warring governments to keep their pledges, and so they went "off the gold standard," i.e., declared their own bankruptcy, shortly after entering the war. All except the United States, which entered the war late, and did not inflate the supply of dollars enough to endanger, redeem ability.

But, apart from the United States, the world suffered what some economists now hail as the Nirvana of freely-fluctuating exchange rates (now called "dirty floats"), competitive devaluations, warring currency blocs, exchange controls, tariffs and quotas, and the breakdown of international trade and investment. The inflated pounds, francs, marks, etc., depreciated in relation to gold and the dollar; monetary chaos abounded throughout the world.

In those days there were, happily, very few economists to hail this situation as the monetary ideal. It was generally recognized that phase II was the threshold to international disaster, and politicians and economists looked around for ways to restore the stability and freedom of the classical gold standard.

Phase III: The Gold-Exchange Standard (Britain and the United States) 1926– 1931

How to return to the Golden Age? The sensible thing to do would have been to recognize the facts of reality, the fact of the depreciated pound, franc, mark, etc., and to return to the gold standard at a redefined rate: a rate that would recognize the existing supply of money and price levels. The British pound, for example, had been traditionally defined at a weight which made it equal to $4.86. But by the end of World War I, the inflation in Britain had brought the pound down to approximately $3.50 on the free foreign-exchange market. Other currencies were similarly depreciated. The sensible policy would have been for Britain to return to gold at approximately $3.50, and for the other inflated countries to do the same. Phase I could have been smoothly and rapidly restored. Instead, the British made the fateful decision to return to gold at the old par of $4.86.

They did so for reasons of British national "prestige," and in a vain attempt to reestablish London as the "hard money" financial center of the world. To succeed at this piece of heroic folly, Britain would have had to deflate severely its money supply and its price levels, for at a $4.86 pound British export prices were far too high to be competitive in the world markets. But deflation was now politically out of the question, for the growth of trade unions, buttressed by a nationwide system of unemployment insurance, had made wage rates rigid downward; in order to deflate, the British government would have had to reverse the growth of its welfare state. In fact, the British wished to continue to inflate money and prices. As a result of combining inflation with a return to an overvalued par, British exports were depressed all during the 1920s and unemployment was severe all during the period when most of the world was experiencing an economic boom.

How could the British try to have their cake and eat it at the same time? By establishing a new international monetary order which would induce or coerce other governments into inflating or into going back to gold at overvalued pars for their own currencies, thus crippling their own exports and subsidizing imports from Britain. This is precisely what Britain did, as it led the way, at the Genoa Conference of 1922, in creating a new international monetary order, the gold- exchange standard.

The gold-exchange standard worked as follows: The United States remained on the classical gold standard, redeeming dollars in gold. Britain and the other countries of the West, however, returned to a pseudo-gold standard, Britain in 1926 and the other countries around the same time. British pounds and other currencies were not payable in gold coins, but only in large-sized bars, suitable only for international transactions. This prevented the ordinary citizens of Britain and other European countries from using gold in their daily life, and thus permitted a wider degree of paper and bank inflation. But furthermore, Britain redeemed pounds not merely in gold, but also in dollars; while the other countries redeemed their currencies not in gold, but in pounds. And most of these countries were induced by Britain to return to gold at overvalued parities. The result was a pyramiding of United States on gold, of British pounds on dollars, and of other European currencies on pounds the "gold-exchange standard," with the dollar and the pound as the two "key currencies."

Now when Britain inflated, and experienced a deficit in its balance of payments, the gold-standard mechanism did not work to quickly restrict British inflation. For instead of other countries redeeming their pounds for gold, they kept the pounds and inflated on top of them.

Hence Britain and Europe were permitted to inflate unchecked, and British deficits could pile up unrestrained by the market discipline of the gold standard. As for the United States, Britain was able to induce the United States to inflate dollars so as not to lose many dollars reserves or gold to the United States.

The point of the gold-exchange standard is that it cannot last; the piper must eventually be paid, but only in a disastrous reaction to the lengthy inflationary boom. As sterling balances piled up in France, the United States, and elsewhere, the slightest loss of confidence in the increasingly shaky and jerry-built inflationary structure was bound to lead to general collapse. This is precisely what happened in 1931; the failure of inflated banks throughout Europe, and the attempt of "hard money" France to cash in its sterling balances for gold, led Britain to go off the gold standard completely. Britain was soon followed by the other countries of Europe.

Phase IV: Fluctuating Fiat Currencies, 1931–1945

The world was now backing to the monetary chaos of World War I, except that now there seemed to be little hope for a restoration of gold. The international economic order had disintegrated into the chaos of clean and dirty floating exchange rates, competing devaluations, exchange controls, and trade barriers; international economic and monetary warfare raged between currencies and currency blocs. International trade and investment came to a virtual standstill; and trade was conducted through barter agreements conducted by governments competing and conflicting with one another. Secretary of State Cordell Hull repeatedly pointed out that these monetary and economic conflicts of the 1930s were the major cause of World War II.

The United States remained on the gold standard for two years, and then, in 1933–1934, went off the classical gold standard in a vain attempt to get out of the depression. American citizens could no longer redeem dollars in gold, and were even prohibited from owning any gold, either here or abroad. But the United States remained, after 1934, on a peculiar new form of gold standard, in which the dollar, now redefined to 1/35 of a gold ounce, was redeemable in gold to foreign governments and central banks. A lingering tie to gold remained. Furthermore, the monetary chaos in Europe led to gold flowing into the only relatively safe monetary haven, the United States.

The chaos and the unbridled economic warfare of the 1930s points up an important lesson: the grievous *political* flaw (apart from the economic problems) in the Milton Friedman-Chicago School monetary scheme for freely-fluctuating fiat currencies. For what the Friedmanites would do *in the name of the free market* is to cut all ties to gold completely, leave the absolute control of each national currency in the hands of its central government issuing fiat paper as legal tender *and then* advise each government to allow its currency to fluctuate freely with respect to all other fiat currencies, as well as to refrain from inflating its currency too outrageously. The grave political flaw is to hand total control of the money supply to the Nation-State, and then to hope and expect that the State will refrain from using that power. And since power always tends to be used, including the power to counterfeit legally, the naiveté, as well as the statist nature, of this type of program should be starkly evident.

And so, the disastrous experience of phase IV, the 1930s world of fiat paper and economic warfare, led the US authorities to adopt as their major economic war aim of World War II the restoration of a viable international monetary order, an order on which could be built a renaissance of world trade and the fruits of the international division of labor.

Phase V: Bretton Woods and the New Gold-Exchange Standard (the United States) 1945–1968

The new international monetary order was conceived and then driven through by the United States at an international monetary conference at Bretton Woods, New Hampshire, in mid-1944, and ratified by the Congress in July, 1945. While the Bretton Woods system worked far better than the disaster of the 1930s, it worked only as another inflationary recrudescence of the gold-exchange standard of the 1920s and like the 1920s the system lived only on borrowed time.

The new system was essentially the gold-exchange standard of the 1920s but with the dollar rudely displacing the British pound as one of the "key currencies." Now the dollar, valued at 1/35 of a gold ounce, was to be the *only* key currency. The other difference from the 1920s was that the dollar was no longer redeemable in gold to American citizens; instead, the 1930's system was continued, with the dollar redeemable in gold *only* to foreign governments and their central banks. No private individuals, only governments, were to be allowed the privilege of redeeming dollars in the world gold currency.

In the Bretton Woods system, the United States pyramided dollars (in paper money and in bank deposits) on top of gold, in which dollars could be redeemed by foreign governments; while all other governments held dollars as their basic reserve and pyramided their currency on top of dollars. And since the United States began the postwar world with a huge stock of gold (approximately $25 billion) there was plenty of play for pyramiding dollar claims on top of it. Furthermore, the system could "work" for a while because all the world's currencies returned to the new system at their pre-World War II pars, most of which were highly overvalued in terms of their inflated and depreciated currencies. The inflated pound sterling, for example, returned at $4.86, even though it was worth far less than that in terms of purchasing power on the market. Since the dollar was artificially undervalued and most other currencies overvalued in 1945, the dollar was made scarce, and the world suffered from a so-called dollar shortage, which the American taxpayer was supposed to be obligated to make up by foreign aid. In short, the export surplus enjoyed by the undervalued American dollar was to be partly financed by the hapless American taxpayer in the form of foreign aid.

"Since 1971, the market price of gold has never been below the old fixed price of $35 an ounce."

There being plenty of room for inflation before retribution could set in, the US government embarked on its postwar policy of continual monetary inflation, a policy it has pursued merrily ever since. By the early 1950s, the continuing American inflation began to turn the tide of international trade. For while the United States was inflating and expanding money and credit, the major European governments, many of them influenced by "Austrian" monetary advisers, pursued a relatively "hard money" policy (e.g., West Germany, Switzerland, France, Italy). Steeply inflationist Britain was compelled by its outflow of dollars to devalue the pound to more realistic levels (for a while it was approximately $2.40).

All this, combined with the increasing productivity of Europe, and later Japan, led to continuing balance-of-payments deficits with the United States. As the 1950s and 1960s wore on, the United States became more and more inflationist, both absolutely and relatively to Japan and Western Europe. But the classical gold- standard check on inflation especially *American* inflation was gone. For the rules of the Bretton Woods game provided that the West European countries had to keep piling up their reserve, and even use these dollars as a base to inflate their own currency and credit.

But as the 1950s and 1960s continued, the harder-money countries of West Europe (and Japan) became restless at being forced to pile up dollars that were now increasingly overvalued instead of undervalued. As the purchasing power and hence the true value of dollars fell, they became increasingly unwanted by foreign governments. But they were locked into a system that was more and more of a nightmare. The American reaction to the European complaints, headed by France and DeGaulle's major monetary adviser, the classical gold-standard economist Jacques Rueff, was merely scorn and brusque dismissal. American politicians and economists simply declared that Europe was *forced* to use the dollar as its currency that it could do nothing about its growing problems, and therefore the United States could keep blithely inflating while pursuing a policy of "benign neglect" toward the international monetary consequences of its own actions.

But Europe did have the legal option of redeeming dollars in gold at $35 an ounce. And as the dollar became increasingly overvalued in terms of hard money currencies and gold, European governments began more and more to exercise that option. The gold-standard check was coming into use; hence gold flowed steadily out of the United States for two decades after the early 1950s, until the US gold stock dwindled over this period from over $20 billion to $9 billion. As dollars kept inflating upon a dwindling gold base, how could the United States keep redeeming foreign dollars in gold the cornerstone of the Bretton Woods system?

These problems did not slow down continued US inflation of dollars and prices, nor the United States policy of "benign neglect," which resulted by the late 1960s in an accelerated pileup of no less than $80 billion in unwanted dollars in Europe (known as Eurodollars). To try to stop European redemption of dollars into gold, the United States exerted intense political pressure on the European governments, similar but on a far larger scale to the British cajoling of France not to redeem its heavy sterling balances until 1931. But economic law has a way, at long last, of catching up with governments, and this is what happened to the inflation-happy US government by the end of the 1960s. The gold-exchange system of Bretton Woods hailed by the US political and economic establishment as permanent and impregnable began to unravel rapidly in 1968.

Phase VI: The Unraveling of Bretton Woods, 1968–1971

As dollars piled up abroad and gold continued to flow outward, the United States found it increasingly difficult to maintain the price of gold at $35 an ounce in the free gold markets at London and Zurich. Thirty-five dollars an ounce was the keystone of the system, and while American citizens have been barred since 1934 from owning gold anywhere in the world, other citizens have enjoyed the freedom to own gold bullion and coin. Hence, one way for individual Europeans to redeem their dollars in gold was to sell their dollars for gold at $35 an ounce in the free gold market. As the dollar kept inflating and depreciating, and as American balance-of-payments deficits continued, Europeans and other private citizens began to accelerate their sales of dollars into gold. In order to keep the dollar at $35 an ounce, the US government was forced to leak out gold from its dwindling stock to support the $35 price at London and Zurich.

A crisis of confidence in the dollar on the free gold markets led the United States to effect a fundamental change in the monetary system in March 1968. The idea was to stop the pesky free gold market from ever again endangering the Bretton Woods arrangement. Hence was born the "two-tier gold market." The idea was that the free gold market could go to blazes; it would be strictly insulated from the real monetary action in the central banks and governments of the world. The United States would no longer try to keep the free-market gold price at $35; it would ignore the free gold market, and it and all the other governments agreed to keep the value of the dollar at $35 an ounce forevermore.

"The two-tier system moved rapidly toward crisis and to the final dissolution of Bretton Woods."

The governments and central banks of the world would henceforth buy no more gold from the "outside" market and would sell no more gold to that market; from now on gold would simply move as counters from one central bank to another, and new gold supplies, free gold market, or private demand for gold would take their own course completely separated from the monetary arrangements of the world.

Along with this, the United States pushed hard for the new launching of a new kind of world paper reserve, Special Drawing Rights (SDRs), which it was hoped would eventually replace gold altogether and serve as a new world paper currency to be issued by a future World Reserve Bank; if such a system were ever established, then the United States could inflate unchecked forevermore, in collaboration with other world governments (the only limit would then be the disastrous one of a worldwide runaway inflation and the crackup of the world paper currency). But the SDRs, combatted intensely as they have been by

Western Europe and the "hard-money" countries, have so far been only a small supplement to American and other currency reserves.

All pro-paper economists, from Keynesians to Friedmanites, were now confident that gold would disappear from the international monetary system; cut off from its "support" by the dollar, these economists all confidently predicted, the free-market gold price would soon fall below $35 an ounce, and even down to the estimated "industrial" nonmonetary gold price of $10 an ounce. Instead, the free price of gold, never below $35, had been steadily above $35, and by early 1973 had climbed to around $125 an ounce, a figure that no pro-paper economist would have thought possible as recently as a year earlier.

Far from establishing a permanent new monetary system, the two-tier gold market only bought a few years of time; American inflation and deficits continued. Eurodollars accumulated rapidly, gold continued to flow outward, and the higher free-market price of gold simply revealed the accelerated loss of world confidence in the dollar. The two-tier system moved rapidly toward crisis and to the final dissolution of Bretton Woods.

Phase VII: The End of Bretton Woods: Fluctuating Fiat Currencies, August– December 1971

On August 15, 1971, at the same time that President Nixon imposed a price-wage freeze in a vain attempt to check bounding inflation, Mr. Nixon also brought the postwar Bretton Woods system to a crashing end. As European central banks at last threatened to redeem much of their swollen stock of dollars for gold, President Nixon went totally off gold. For the first time in American history, the dollar was totally fiat, totally without backing in gold. Even the tenuous link with gold maintained since 1933 was now severed. The world was plunged into the fiat system of the 1930s and worse, since now even the dollar was no longer linked to gold. Ahead loomed the dread spectre of currency blocs, competing devaluations, economic warfare, and the breakdown of international trade and investment, with the worldwide depression that would then ensue.

What to do? Attempting to restore an international monetary order lacking a link to gold, the United States led the world into the Smithsonian Agreement on December 18, 1971.

Phase VIII: The Smithsonian Agreement, December 1971–February 1973

The Smithsonian Agreement, hailed by President Nixon as the "greatest monetary agreement in the history of the world," was even more shaky and unsound than the gold-exchange standard of the 1920s or than Bretton Woods. For once again, the countries of the world pledged to maintain fixed exchange rates, but this time with no gold or world money to give any currency backing. Furthermore, many European currencies were fixed at undervalued parities in relation to the dollar; the only US concession was a puny devaluation of the official dollar rate to $38 an ounce. But while much too little and too late, this devaluation was significant in violating an endless round of official American pronouncements, which had pledged to maintain the $35 rate forevermore. Now at last the $35 price was implicitly acknowledged as not graven on tablets of stone.

It was inevitable that fixed exchange rates, even with wider agreed zones of fluctuation, but lacking a world medium of exchange, were doomed to rapid defeat. This was especially true since American inflation of money and prices, the decline of the dollar, and balance-of-payments deficits continued unchecked.

The swollen supply of Eurodollars, combined with the continued inflation and the removal of gold backing, drove the free-market gold price up to $215 an ounce. And as the overvaluation of the dollar and the undervaluation of European and Japanese hard money became increasingly evident, the dollar finally broke apart on the world markets in the panic months of February–March 1973. It became impossible for West Germany, Switzerland, France and the other hard money countries to continue to buy dollars in order to support the dollar at an overvalued rate. In little over a year, the Smithsonian system of fixed exchange rates without gold had smashed apart on the rocks of economic reality.

Phase IX: Fluctuating Fiat Currencies, March 1973–?

With the dollar breaking apart, the world shifted again, to a system of fluctuating fiat currencies. Within the West European bloc, exchange rates were tied to one another, and the United States again devalued the official dollar rate by a token amount to $42 an ounce. As the dollar plunged in foreign exchange from day to day, and the West German mark, the Swiss franc, and the Japanese yen hurtled upward, the American authorities, backed by the Friedmanite economists, began to think that this was the monetary ideal. It is true that dollar surpluses and sudden balance-of-payments crises do not plague the world under fluctuating exchange rates. Furthermore, American export firms began to chortle that falling dollar rates made American goods cheaper abroad, and therefore benefitted exports. It is true that governments persisted in interfering with exchange fluctuations ("dirty" instead of "clean" floats), but overall, it seemed that the international monetary order had sundered into a Friedmanite utopia.

But it became clear all too soon that all is far from well in the current international monetary system. The long-run problem is that the hard-money countries will not sit by forever and watch their currencies become more expensive and their exports hurt for the benefit of their American competitors. If American inflation and dollar depreciation continues, they will soon shift to the competing devaluation, exchange controls, currency blocs, and economic warfare of the 1930s.

But more immediate is the other side of the coin: the fact that depreciating dollars means that American imports are far more expensive, American tourists suffer abroad, and cheap exports are snapped up by foreign countries so rapidly as to raise prices of exports at home (e.g., the American wheat-and-meat price inflation). So that American exporters might indeed benefit, but only at the expense of the inflation-ridden American consumer. The crippling uncertainty of rapid exchange-rate fluctuations was brought starkly home to Americans with the rapid plunge of the dollar in foreign-exchange markets in July 1973.

Since the United States went completely off gold in August 1971 and established the Friedmanite fluctuating fiat system in March 1973, the United States and the world have suffered the most intense and most sustained bout of peacetime inflation in the history of the world. It should be clear by now that this is scarcely a coincidence. Before the dollar was cut loose from gold, Keynesians and Friedmanites, each in their own way devoted to fiat paper money, confidently predicted that when fiat money was established, the market price of gold would fall promptly to its nonmonetary level, then estimated at about $8 an ounce.

In their scorn of gold, both groups maintained that it was the mighty dollar that was propping up the price of gold, and not vice versa. Since 1971, the market price of gold has never been below the old, fixed price of $35 an ounce, and has almost always been enormously higher. When, during the 1950s and 1960s, economists such as Jacques Rueff were calling for a gold standard at a price of $70 an ounce, the price was considered absurdly high. It is now even more absurdly low. The far higher gold price is an indication of the calamitous deterioration of the dollar since "modern" economists had their way and all gold backing was removed.

It is now all too clear that the world has become fed up with the unprecedented inflation, in the United States and throughout the world that has been sparked by the fluctuating fiat currency era inaugurated in 1973. We are also weary of the extreme volatility and unpredictability of currency exchange rates. This volatility is the consequence of the national fiat-money system, which fragmented the world's money and added artificial political instability to the natural uncertainty in the free-market price system. The Friedmanite dream of fluctuating fiat money lies in ashes, and there is an understandable yearning to return to international money with fixed exchange rates.

Unfortunately, the classical gold standard lies forgotten, and the ultimate goal of most American and world leaders is the old Keynesian vision of a one-world fiat paper standard, a new currency unit issued by a World Reserve Bank (WRB). Whether the new currency be termed "the bancor" (offered by Keynes), the "unita" (proposed by World War II US Treasury official Harry Dexter White), or the "phoenix" (suggested by The Economist) is unimportant. The vital point is that such an international paper currency, while indeed free of balance-of-payments crises (since the WRB could issue as much bancors as it wished and supply them to its country of choice), would provide for an open channel for unlimited world- wide inflation, unchecked by either balance-of-payments crises or by declines in exchange rates.

The WRB would then be the all-powerful determinant of the world's money supply and its national distribution. The WRB could and would subject the world to what it believes will be a wisely-controlled inflation. Unfortunately, there would then be nothing standing in the way of the unimaginably catastrophic economic holocaust of world-wide runaway inflation, nothing, that is, except the dubious capacity of the WRB to fine-tune the world economy.

While a world-wide paper unit and central bank remain the ultimate goal of world's Keynesian-oriented leaders, the more realistic and proximate goal is a return to a glorified Bretton Woods scheme, except this time without the check of any backing in gold. Already the world's major central banks are attempting to "coordinate" monetary and economic policies, harmonize rates of inflation, and fix exchange rates. The militant drive for a European paper currency issued by a European central bank seems on the verge of success. This goal is being sold to the gullible public by the fallacious claim that a free-trade European Economic Community (EEC) necessarily requires an overarching European bureaucracy, a uniformity of taxation throughout the EEC, and, in particular, a European central bank and paper unit. Once that is achieved, closer coordination with the Federal Reserve and other major central banks will follow immediately. And then, could a World Central Bank be far behind? Short of that ultimate goal, however, we may soon be plunged into yet another Bretton Woods, with all the attendant crises of the balance of payments and Gresham's Law that follow from fixed exchange rates in a world of fiat moneys.

As we face the future, the prognosis for the dollar and for the international monetary system is grim indeed. Until and unless we return to the classical gold standard at a realistic gold price, the international money system is fated to shift back and forth between fixed and fluctuating exchange rates with each system posing unsolved problems, working badly, and finally disintegrating. And fueling this disintegration will be the continued inflation of the supply of dollars and hence of American prices which show no sign of abating. The prospect for the future is accelerating and eventually runaway inflation at home, accompanied by monetary breakdown and economic warfare abroad. This prognosis can only be changed by a drastic alteration of the American and world monetary system: by the return to a free market commodity money such as gold and by removing government totally from the monetary scene.

Murray N. Rothbard (1926–1995) was dean of the Austrian School. He was an economist, economic historian, and libertarian political philosopher. See Murray
N. Rothbard's.

Notes

For a recent study of the classical gold standard, and a history of the early phases of its breakdown in the 20th century, see Melchior Palyi, *The Twilight of Gold, 1914–1936* (Chicago: Henry Regnery, 1972).

On the crucial British error and its consequence in leading to the 1929 depression, see Lionel Robbins, *The Great Depression* (New York: Macmillan, 1934).

Cordell Hull, *Memoirs* (New York, 1948), vol. I, p. 81. Also see Richard N. Gardner,
Sterling-Dollar Conspiracy (Oxford: Clarendon Press, 1956), p. 141.

On the two-tier gold market, see Jacques Rueff, *The Monetary Sin of the West*
(New York: Macmillan, 1972).

Chapter 14

Communists in The Shadows 1963

There is relentless effort to Change America and the Points of 45

Turning Points

You are about to read a list of 45 goals that found their way down the halls of our great Capitol back in 1963. As you read this you should be shocked by the events that have played themselves out.

Communist Goals (1963) Congressional Record Appendix, pp. A34-A35 January 10, 1963

Current Communist Goals EXTENSION OF REMARKS OF HON. A. S. HERLONG, JR. OF FLORIDA IN THE HOUSE OF REPRESENTATIVES Thursday, January 10, 1963.

Mr. HERLONG. Mr. Speaker, Mrs. Patricia Nordman of De Land, Fla., is an ardent and articulate opponent of communism, and until recently published the De Land Courier, which she dedicated to the purpose of alerting the public to the dangers of communism in America.

At Mrs. Nordman's request, I include in the RECORD, under unanimous consent, the following "Current Communist Goals," which she identifies as an excerpt from "The Naked Communist," by Cleon Skousen:
[From "The Naked Communist," by Cleon Skousen]

1. U.S. acceptance of coexistence as the only alternative to atomic war.

2. U.S. willingness to capitulate in preference to engaging in atomic war.

3. Develop the illusion that total disarmament [by] the United States would be a demonstration of moral strength.

4. Permit free trade between all nations regardless of Communist affiliation and regardless of whether or not items could be used for war.

5. Extension of long-term loans to Russia and Soviet satellites.

6. Provde American aid to all nations regardless of Communist domination.

7. Grant recognition of Red China. Admission of Red China to the U.N.

8. Set up East and West Germany as separate states in spite of Khrushchev's promise in 1955 to settle the German question by free elections under supervision of the U.N.

9. Prolong the conferences to ban atomic tests because the United States has agreed to suspend tests as long as negotiations are in progress.

10. Allow all Soviet satellites individual representation in the U.N.

11. Promote the U.N. as the only hope for mankind. If its charter is rewritten, demand that it be set up as a one-world government with its own independent armed forces. (Some Communist leaders believe the world can be taken over as easily by the U.N. as by Moscow. Sometimes these two centers compete with each other as they are now doing in the Congo.)

12. Resist any attempt to outlaw the Communist Party.

13. Do away with all loyalty oaths.

14. Continue giving Russia access to the U.S. Patent Office.

15. Capture one or both of the political parties in the United States.

16. Use technical decisions of the courts to weaken basic American institutions by claiming their activities violate civil rights.

17. Get control of the schools. Use them as transmission belts for socialism and current Communist propaganda. Soften the curriculum. Get control of teachers' associations. Put the party line in textbooks.

18. Gain control of all student newspapers.

19. Use student riots to foment public protests against programs or organizations which are under Communist attack.

20. Infiltrate the press. Get control of book-review assignments, editorial writing, and policy-making positions.

21. Gain control of key positions in radio, TV, and motion pictures.

22. Continue discrediting American culture by degrading all forms of artistic expression. An American Communist cell was told to "eliminate all good sculpture from parks and buildings, substitute shapeless, awkward and meaningless forms."

23. Control art critics and directors of art museums. "Our plan is to promote ugliness, repulsive, meaningless art."

24. Eliminate all laws governing obscenity by calling them "censorship" and a violation of free speech and free press.

25. Break down cultural standards of morality by promoting

pornography and obscenity in books, magazines, motion pictures, radio, and TV.

26. Present homosexuality, degeneracy and promiscuity as "normal, natural, and healthy."

27. Infiltrate the churches and replace revealed religion with "social" religion. Discredit the Bible and emphasize the need for intellectual maturity, which does not need a "religious crutch."

28. Eliminate prayer or any phase of religious expression in the schools on the ground that it violates the principle of "separation of church and state."

29. Discredit the American Constitution by calling it inadequate, old-fashioned, out of step with modern needs, a hindrance to cooperation between nations on a worldwide basis.

30. 30. Discredit the American Founding Fathers. Present them as selfish aristocrats who had no concern for the "common man."

31. Belittle all forms of American culture and discourage the teaching of American history on the ground that it was only a minor part of the "big picture." Give more emphasis to Russian history since the Communists took over.

32. Support any socialist movement to give centralized control over any part of the culture education, social agencies, welfare programs, mental health clinics, etc.

33. Eliminate all laws or procedures which interfere with the operation of the Communist apparatus.

34. Eliminate the House Committee on Un-American Activities.

35. Discredit and eventually dismantle the FBI.

36. Infiltrate and gain control of more unions.

37. Infiltrate and gain control of big business.

38. Transfer some of the powers of arrest from the police to social agencies. Treat all behavioral problems as psychiatric disorders which no one but psychiatrists can understand [or treat].

39. Dominate the psychiatric profession and use mental health laws as a means of gaining coercive control over those who oppose Communist goals.

40. Discredit the family as an institution. Encourage promiscuity and easy divorce.

41. Emphasize the need to raise children away from the negative influence of parents. Attribute prejudices, mental blocks and retarding of children to suppressive influence of parents.

42. Create the impression that violence and insurrection are legitimate aspects of the American tradition; that students and special-interest groups should rise up and use ["] united force ["] to solve economic, political or social problems.

43. Overthrow all colonial governments before native populations are ready for self-government.

44. Internationalize the Panama Canal.

45. Repeal the Connelly reservation so the United States cannot prevent the World Court from seizing jurisdiction [over domestic problems. Give the World Court jurisdiction] over nations and individuals alike.

It will probably be available at your nearest library that is a federal repository. Call them and ask them. Your college library is probably a repository. This is an excellent source of government records. Another source are your Congress Critters. They should be more than happy to help you in this matter. You will find the Ten Planks of the Communist

Manifesto interesting at this point.

Sources are listed below.

Microfilm: California State University at San Jose Clark Library, Government Floor Phone (408)924-2770 Microfilm Call Number: J 11.R5

Congressional Record, Vol. 109 88th Congress, 1st Session Appendix Pages A1- A2842 Jan. 9-May 7, 1963 Reel 12

1963- The Year That Changed America

By Greg Swank

12-4-2

Over the years, I have shared in debates and discussions regarding the current state of affairs in the U.S., and the changing social climate of this great nation. Since the "baby-boomer" generation, society and its culture have become noticeably different than the way it was 50 years ago. From the late 50's to the 70's a series of events took place contributing to the way we are currently living. However, like anything else, there has to be a starting point at which the wheels are put into motion. Sometimes it can be a single event, such as war, but more often, it is a series of events, some intentional, some planned, others unpredictable. There is always a pivotal point when things begin to change. I believe that time was 1963.

For my generation, some of the following will certainly stir old memories. If you were born later, this may serve as a brief history lesson into the times your parents traveled through.

By 1963 television was the leading sources of entertainment. The public enjoyed a different type of programming back then. Lessons on life could be viewed weekly on "Leave it to Beaver" or "My Three Sons." There were hero's back then that never drew blood, "The Lone Ranger" and "The Adventures of Superman." Cartoon series evolved, such as, "The Flintstones" and "The Jetsons" without messages of empowering the children, using vulgarities or demeaning parental guidance. Family's could spend a weekend evening watching "Ed Sullivan," "Bonanza" or "Gun Smoke." For those who enjoyed the thrill and suspense, we were blessed with "Alfred Hitchcock Presents" and the "Twilight Zone." 'My Favorite Martian," "Ozzie and Harriet," "Donna Reed" and "Sea Hunt" also kept viewers entertained weekly.

Movie theaters were not multiplex units with 15 screens, rather, one single, giant big screen with adequate sound and hard seats without springs. "Tom Jones" had won the Academy award for best picture.

"How The West Was Won," "Cleopatra," "Lily of the Fields," "The Great Escape," "The Birds," and "It's a Mad, Mad, Mad, Mad World" were all box office hits.

By year's end, "The Beatles" had played for the British Royal Family and were laying the groundwork to conquer the U.S. the following year. Eric Clapton began his journey to fame with Jeff Beck, Jimmy Page, Jim McCarty and their band, "The Yard birds." Out on the west coast the surf was beginning to rock-n-roll with "The Beach Boys" and their first song to reach the top ten list, "Surfing' U.S.A."

"Joys of Jell-O" recipes for quivering florescent foodstuff hit the stores. U.S. Postal rates went up to five cents for the first ounce. AT&T introduced touch-tone telephones. The Yankees played in the World Series again; but lost to the Dodgers in four straight. The government and NASA began the Apollo program.

This is just a brief snapshot of some things that were going on back in 1963. Remember?

While some of these events played an important role in the direction of change that affect us today, many of them were lost to much greater, more political events, that I believe put everything into motion.

On January 10, 1963, the House of Representative and later the Senate began reviewing a document entitled "Communist Goals for Taking over America." It contained an agenda of 45 separate issues that, in hindsight was quite shocking back then and equally shocking today. Here, in part, are some key points listed in that document.

4. Permit free trade between all nations regardless of Communist affiliation and regardless of whether or not items could be used for war.

5. Extension of long-term loans to Russia and Soviet satellites.

8. Set up East and West Germany as separate states.11. Promote the U.N. as the only hope for mankind.

13. Do away with all loyalty oaths.

16. Use technical decisions of the courts to weaken basic American institutions by claiming their activities violate civil rights.

23. Control art critics and directors of art museums. "Our plan is to promote ugliness, repulsive, meaningless art."

24. Eliminate all laws governing obscenity by calling them "censorship" and a violation of free speech and free press.

25. Break down cultural standards of morality by promoting pornography and obscenity in books, magazines, motion pictures, radio, and TV.

26. Present homosexuality, degeneracy, and promiscuity as "normal, natural, and healthy."

27. Discredit the Bible and emphasize the need for intellectual maturity, which does not need a "religious crutch."

28. Eliminate prayer or any phase of religious expression in the schools on the ground that it violates the principle of "separation of church and state."

40. Discredit the family as an institution. Encourage promiscuity and easy divorce.

44. Internationalize the Panama Canal.

You can see the entire list on this webpage – http://www.thruthtrek. net/politics/takeover

Now, I am not saying that the U.S. is under Communist control, but what I do find frightening, is of the 45 issues listed, nearly all of them have come to pass. Remember this was in January 1963.

In 1963 the news media showed women burning their bras as the women's liberation movement took off with the publishing of "The Feminine Mystique" by Betty Friedan. Martin Luther King was jailed in April and civil unrest was being brought to the forefront. On August 28th the media brought us live coverage of the march on Washington and Dr. Kings famous "I had a dream" speech. The Cuban missile crisis found its way into our homes and our nation was gearing up for conflict.

By September of 1963 we had lost some very influential people, Pope John XXIII, Robert Frost, and country legend Patsy Cline, to name a few. In the early hours of November 22nd, we learned of the quiet passing of C.S. Lewis and hours later we were brought to our knees when President John F. Kennedy was assassinated and our nation mourned.

So you see, while long since forgotten, 1963 could very well have been, one of the most important years since our founding fathers provided us with the Constitution of the United States. Which brings me to one final and extremely important decision that was made during this most provocative year?

On June 17, 1963, the U.S. Supreme Court concluded that any Bible reciting or prayer, in public schools, was deemed unconstitutional.

While American's have endured great prosperity over the past 40 years, we have also lost our moral compass and direction. In reviewing the research, data supports 1963 as a focal point, demonstrating a downward slope in our moral and social decline through 2001 to 2011.

Certainly, one would have to agree that all these events have had a profound impact on the way our current social structure has been changed. Personally, if I had to choose one specific event that has demonstrated the demoralization of our country, it would have to be the decision of the U.S Supreme Court in June of 1963.

But this is not all that has transpired since 1963. We currently have among us the Democratic Socialist of Congress. They hide behind the word Socialist when their true motives are directed as Communists. The list is below:

Co-Chairs Hon. Raúl M. Grijalva (AZ-07) Hon. Lynn Woolsey (CA-06) Vice Chairs Hon. Diane Watson (CA-

Hon. Sheila Jackson-Lee (TX-18) Hon. Mazie Hirono (HI-02) Hon. Dennis Kucinich (OH-10) Senate Members Hon. Bernie Sanders (VT) House Members Hon. Neil Abercrombie (HI-01) Hon. Tammy Baldwin (WI-02) Hon. Xavier Becerra (CA-31) Hon. Madeleine Bordallo (GU-AL) Hon. Robert Brady (PA-Hon. Corrine Brown (FL-03) Hon. Michael Capuano (MA-08) Hon. André Carson (IN-07) Hon. Donna Christensen (VI-AL) Hon. Yvette Clarke (NY-11) Hon. William "Lacy" Clay (MO-01) Hon. Emanuel Cleaver (MO-05) Hon. Steve Cohen (TN-09) Hon. John Conyers (MI-14) Hon. Elijah Cummings (MD-07) Hon. Danny Davis (IL-07) Hon. Peter DeFazio (OR-04) Hon. Rosa DeLauro (CT-03) Rep. Donna F. Edwards (MD-04) Hon. Keith Ellison (MN-05) Hon. Sam Farr (CA-17) Hon. Chaka Fattah (PA-02) Hon. Bob Filner (CA-51) Hon. Barney Frank (MA-04) Hon. Marcia L. Fudge (OH-11) Hon. Alan Grayson (FL-08) Hon. Luis Gutierrez (IL-04) Hon. John Hall (NY-19) Hon. Phil Hare (IL-17) Hon. Maurice Hinchey (NY-22) Hon. Michael Honda (CA-15) Hon. Jesse Jackson, Jr. (IL-02) Hon. Eddie Bernice Johnson (TX-30) Hon. Hank Johnson (GA-04) Hon. Marcy Kaptur (OH-09) Hon. Carolyn Kilpatrick (MI-13) Hon. Barbara Lee (CA-09) Hon. John Lewis (GA-05) Hon. David Loebsack (IA-02) Hon. Ben R. Lujan (NM-3) Hon. Carolyn Maloney (NY-14) Hon. Ed Markey (MA-07) Hon. Jim McDermott (WA-07) Hon. James

McGovern (MA-03) Hon. George Miller (CA-07) Hon. Gwen Moore (WI-04) Hon. Jerrold Nadler (NY-08) Hon. Eleanor Holmes-Norton (DC-AL) Hon. John Olver (MA-01) Hon. Ed Pastor (AZ-04) Hon. Donald Payne (NJ-10) Hon. Chellie Pingree (ME-01) Hon. Charles Rangel (NY-15) Hon. Laura Richardson (CA-37) Hon. Lucille Roybal-Allard (CA-34) Hon. Bobby Rush (IL-01) Hon. Linda Sánchez (CA-47) Hon. Jan Schakowsky (IL-09) Hon. José Serrano (NY-16) Hon. Louise Slaughter (NY-28) Hon. Pete Stark (CA-13) Hon. Bennie Thompson (MS-02) Hon. John Tierney (MA-06) Hon. Nydia Velazquez (NY-12) Hon. Maxine Waters (CA-35) Hon. Mel Watt (NC-12) Hon. Henry Waxman (CA-30) Hon. Peter Welch (VT-AL) Hon. Robert Wexler (FL-19)

If we look of the events past and current, then what will soon come to pass by LBJ and what he does will drive a knife in the heart of all Americas for generations.

There are intruders in our Liberty and the only way to resolve the issue is to flush them out, expose them with all their motives and cleans the Republic of all their vial attributes and intensions.

Chapter 15

The Great Society The 36th President Lyndon B. Johnson

Turning Points

LBJ served this country from November 22nd, 1963 – January 20th, 1969

He took office after President John F. Kennedy was assassinated in Dallas, Texas. That is another story all unto itself.

Johnson created the Great Society which was another Turning Point in our History.

The *Great Society* was a set of domestic programs proposed or enacted in the United States on the initiative of President Lyndon B. Johnson. Two main goals of the Great Society social reforms were the elimination of poverty and racial injustice. New major spending programs that addressed education, medical care, urban problems, and transportation were launched during this period. The Great Society in scope and sweep resembled the New Deal domestic agenda of Franklin D. Roosevelt but differed sharply in types of programs enacted.

Some Great Society proposals were stalled initiatives from John F. Kennedy's New Frontier. Johnson's success depended on his skills of persuasion, coupled with the Democratic landslide in the 1964 election that brought in many new liberals to Congress. Anti-war Democrats complained that spending on the Vietnam War choked off the Great Society. While some of the programs have been eliminated or had their funding reduced, many of them, including Medicare, Medicaid, and federal education funding, continue to the present. The Great Society's programs expanded under the administrations of Richard Nixon and Gerald Ford.

Johnson created the War on Poverty:

War on Poverty:

The most ambitious and controversial part of the Great Society was its initiative to end poverty. The Kennedy Administration had been contemplating a federal effort against poverty. Johnson, who as a teacher had observed extreme poverty in Texas among Mexican-Americans, launched an "unconditional war on poverty" in the first months of his presidency with the goal of eliminating hunger and deprivation from American life. The centerpiece of the War on Poverty was the Economic Opportunity Act of 1964, which created an Office of Economic Opportunity (OEO) to oversee a variety of community-based antipoverty programs. The OEO reflected a fragile consensus among policymakers that the best way to deal with poverty was not simply to raise the incomes of the poor but to help them better themselves through education, job training, and community development. Central to its mission was the idea of "community action," the participation of the poor in framing and administering the programs designed to help them.

The War on Poverty began with a $1 billion appropriation in 1964 and spent another $2 billion in the following two years. It spawned dozens of programs, among them the Job Corps, whose purpose was to help disadvantaged youth develop marketable skills; the Neighborhood Youth Corps, established to give poor urban youths work experience and to encourage them to stay in school; Volunteers in Service to America (VISTA), a domestic version of the Peace Corps, which placed concerned citizens with community-based agencies to work towards empowerment of the poor; the Model Cities Program for urban redevelopment; Upward Bound, which assisted poor high school students entering college; legal services for the poor; the Food Stamps program; the Community Action Program, which initiated local Community Action Agencies charged with helping the poor become self-sufficient; and Project Head Start, which offered preschool education for poor children.

Education:

The most important educational component of the Great Society was the Elementary and Secondary Education Act of 1965, designed by Commissioner of Education Francis Keppel. It was signed into law on April 11, 1965, less than three months after it was introduced. It ended a long-standing political taboo by providing significant federal aid to public education, initially allotting more than

$1 billion to help schools purchase materials and start special education programs to schools with a high concentration of low-income children. The Act established Head Start, which had originally been started by the Office of Economic Opportunity as an eight-week summer program, as a permanent program.

Higher Education Act of 1965 increased federal money given to universities, created scholarships and low-interest loans for students, and established a National Teachers Corps to provide teachers to poverty stricken areas of the United States. It began a transition from federally funded institutional assistance to individual student aid.

The Bilingual Education Act of 1968 offered federal aid to local school districts in assisting them to address the needs of children with limited English-speaking ability until it expired in 2002.

Medicare:

The Social Security Act of 1965 authorized Medicare and provided federal funding for many of the medical costs of older Americans. The legislation overcame the bitter resistance, particularly from the American Medical Association, to the idea of publicly-funded health care or "socialized medicine" by making its benefits available to everyone over sixty-five, regardless of need, and by linking payments to the existing private insurance system.

Medicaid:

In 1966 welfare recipients of all ages received medical care through the Medicaid program. Medicaid was created on July 30, 1965 through Title XIX of the Social Security Act. Each state administers its own Medicaid program while the federal Centers for Medicare and Medicaid Services (CMS) monitors the state-run programs and establishes requirements for service delivery, quality, funding, and eligibility standards.

Arts and cultural institutions:

National endowments for arts and humanities:

In September 1965, Johnson signed the National Foundation on the Arts and Humanities Act into law, creating both the National Endowment for the Arts and National Endowment for the Humanities as separate, independent agencies. Lobbying for federally funded arts and humanities support began during the Kennedy Administration. In 1963 three scholarly and educational organizations the American Council of Learned Societies (ACLS), the Council of Graduate Schools in America, and the United Chapters of Phi Beta Kappa joined together to establish the National Commission on the Humanities. In June 1964 the commission released a report that suggested that the emphasis placed on science endangered the study of the humanities from elementary schools through postgraduate programs. In order to correct the balance, it recommended "the establishment by the President and the Congress of the United States of a National Humanities Foundation." In August 1964, Congressman William Moorhead of Pennsylvania proposed legislation to implement the commission's recommendations. Support from the White House followed in September, when Johnson lent his endorsement during a speech at Brown University. In March 1965, the White House proposed the establishment a National Foundation on the Arts and Humanities and requested $20 million in start-up funds. The commission's report had generated other proposals, but the White House's approach eclipsed them. The administration's plan, which called for the creation of two separate agencies each, advised by a governing body, was the version approved by Congress. Richard Nixon dramatically expanded funding for NEH and NEA.

Public broadcasting:

After the First National Conference on Long-Range Financing of Educational Television Stations in December 1964 called for a study of the role of noncommercial education television in society, the Carnegie Corporation agreed to finance the work of a 15-member national commission. Its landmark report, *Public Television: a Program for Action*, published on January 26, 1967, popularized the phrase "public television" and assisted the legislative campaign for federal aid. The Public Broadcasting Act of 1967, enacted less than 10 months later, chartered the Corporation for Public Broadcasting as a private, non-profit corporation. The law initiated federal aid through the CPB for the operation, as opposed to the funding of capital facilities, of public broadcasting. The CPB initially collaborated with the pre-existing National Educational Television system, but in 1969 decided to start the Public Broadcasting Service (PBS). A public radio study commissioned by the CPB and the Ford Foundation and conducted from 1968-1969 led to the establishment of National Public Radio, a public radio system under the terms of the amended Public Broadcasting Act.

Cultural centers:

Two long-planned national cultural and arts facilities received federal funding that would allow for their completion through Great Society legislation. A National Cultural Center, suggested during the Franklin Roosevelt Administration and created by a bipartisan law signed by Dwight Eisenhower, was transformed into the John F. Kennedy Center for the Performing Arts, a living memorial to the assassinated president. Fundraising for the original cultural center had been poor prior to legislation creating the Kennedy Center, which passed two months after the president's death and provided $23 million for construction. The Kennedy Center opened in 1971. In the late 1930s the United States Congress mandated a Smithsonian Institution art museum for the National Mall, and a design by Eliel Saarinen was unveiled in 1939, but plans were shelved during World War II. An 1966 act of Congress established the Hirshhorn Museum and Sculpture Garden as part of the Smithsonian Institution with a focus on modern art, in contrast to the existing National Art Gallery. The museum was primarily federally funded, although New York financier Joseph Hirshhorn later contributed $1 million toward building construction, which began in 1969. The Hirshhorn opened in 1974.

Transportation:

The most sweeping reorganization of the federal government since the National Security Act of 1947 was the consolidation of transportation agencies into a cabinet-level Department of Transportation. The department was authorized by Congress on October 15, 1966 and began operations on April 1, 1967. The Urban Mass Transportation Act of 1964 provided $375 million for large-scale urban public or private rail projects in the form of matching funds to cities and states and created the Urban Mass Transit Administration (now the Federal Transit Administration). The National Traffic and Motor Vehicle Safety

Act of 1966 and the Highway Safety Act of 1966 were enacted, largely as a result of Ralph Nader's book *Unsafe at Any Speed.*

Consumer protection:

In 1964 Johnson named Assistant Secretary of Labor Esther Peterson to be the first presidential assistant for consumer affairs.

Cigarette Labeling Act of 1965 required packages to carry warning labels. Motor Vehicle Safety Act of 1966 set standards through creation of the National Highway Traffic Safety Administration. Fair Packaging and Labeling Act requires products identify manufacturer, address, clearly mark quantity and servings. Statute also authorizes permits HEW and FTC to establish and define voluntary standard sizes. The original would have mandated uniform standards of size and weight for comparison shopping, but the final law only outlawed exaggerated size claims. Child Safety Act of 1966 prohibited any chemical so dangerous that no warning can make it safe. Flammable Fabrics Act of 1967 set standards for children's sleepwear, but not baby blankets. Wholesome Meat Act of 1967 required inspection of meat which must meet federal standards. Truth-in-Lending Act of 1968 required lenders and credit providers to disclose the full cost of finance charges in both dollars and annual percentage rates, on installment loan and sales. Wholesome Poultry Products Act of 1968 required inspection of poultry which must meet federal standards. Land Sales Disclosure Act of 1968 provided safeguards against fraudulent practices in the sale of land. Radiation Safety Act of 1968 provided standards and recalls for defective electronic products.

Environment:

Joseph A. Califano, Jr. has suggested that the Great Society's main contribution to the environment was an extension of protections beyond those aimed at the conservation of untouched resources. Discussing his administration's environmental policies, Lyndon Johnson suggested that "the air we breathe, our water, our soil and wildlife, are being blighted by poisons and chemicals which are the by-products of technology and industry. The society that receives the rewards of technology, must, as a cooperating whole, take responsibility for [their] control. To deal with these new problems will require a new conservation. We must not only protect the countryside and save it from destruction; we must restore what has been destroyed and salvage the beauty and charm of our cities. Our conservation must be not just the classic conservation of protection and development, but a creative conservation of restoration and innovation." At the behest of Secretary of the Interior Stewart Udall, the Great Society included several new environmental laws to protect air and water. Environmental legislation enacted included:

- Clear Air, Water Quality and Clean Water Restoration Acts and Amendments

- Wilderness Act of 1964,

- Endangered Species Preservation Act of 1966,

- National Trails System Act of 1968,

- Wild and Scenic Rivers Act of 1968,

- Land and Water Conservation Act of 1965,

- Solid Waste Disposal Act of 1965,

- Motor Vehicle Air Pollution Control Act of 1965,

- National Historic Preservation Act of 1966,

- Aircraft Noise Abatement Act of 1968, and

- National Environmental Policy Act of 1969.

The legacies of the Great Society:

Several observers have noted that funding for many Great Society programs, particularly the poverty initiatives, became difficult beginning in 1968, chiefly due to the Vietnam War and Johnson's desire to maintain a balanced budget. Many Great Society initiatives, especially those that benefited the middle class, continue to exist in some form. Civil rights laws remain on the books in amended versions. Some programs, like Medicare and Medicaid, have been criticized as inefficient and unwieldy, but enjoy wide support and have grown considerably since the 1960s. Federal funding of public and higher education has expanded since the Great Society era and has maintained bipartisan support. Federal funding for culture initiatives in the arts, humanities, and public broadcasting have repeatedly been targets for elimination, but have survived.

The War on Poverty:

Interpretations of the War on Poverty remain controversial. The Office of Economic Opportunity was dismantled by the Nixon and Ford administrations, largely by transferring poverty programs to other government departments.

Funding for many of these programs were further cut in President Ronald Reagan's first budget in 1981.

Alan Brinkley has suggested that "the gap between the expansive intentions of the War on Poverty and its relatively modest achievements fueled later conservative arguments that government is not an appropriate vehicle for solving social problems." The poverty programs were heavily criticized by conservatives like Charles Murray, who denounced them in his 1984 book *Losing Ground* as being ineffective and creating an underclass of lazy citizens. One of Johnson's aides Joseph A. Califano, Jr. has countered that "from 1963 when Lyndon Johnson took office until 1970 as the impact of his Great Society programs were felt, the portion of Americans living below the poverty line dropped from 22.2 percent to 12.6 percent, the most dramatic decline over such a brief period in this century." The percentage of

African Americans below the poverty line dropped from 55 percent in 1960 to 27 percent in 1968.

Conservative economist Thomas Sowell argues that the Great Society programs only contributed to the destruction of African American families, saying "the black family, which had survived centuries of slavery and discrimination, began rapidly disintegrating into the liberal welfare state that subsidized unwed pregnancy and changed welfare from an emergency rescue to a way of life." Professor William L. Anderson also criticized the War on Poverty, noting the increase of dependency on the government as being harmful to the lower classes."

Neoconservatives:

Irving Kristol and other critics of Great Society programs founded a politics and culture journal The Public Interest in 1965. While most of these critics had been anti-communist liberals, their writings were skeptical of the perceived social engineering of the Great Society. Although retaining much of their big government attitude and interventionist philosophy, because of this opposition to a specific aspect of Liberalism, they came to refer to themselves as neo- conservatives.

References:

Bibliography:

- John A. Andrew *Lyndon Johnson and the Great Society:* I.R. Dee, 1998   ISBN 1-56663-184-X

- Eli Ginzberg and Robert M. Solow (eds.) *The Great Society: Lessons for the Future* ISBN 0-465-02705-9 (1974), 11 chapters on each program, by experts

- Jeffrey W. Helsing J*ohnson's War/Johnson's Great Society: the guns and butter trap* Praeger Greenwood 2000 ISBN 0-275-96449-3

- Marshall Kaplan and Peggy L. Cuciti; *The Great Society and Its Legacy: Twenty Years of U.S. Social Policy* Duke University Press, 1986 ISBN 0-8223- 0589-5

- Barbara C. Jordan and Elspeth D. Rostow (editors) *The Great Society: a twenty year critique*: Lyndon B. Johnson School of Public Affairs 1986 ISBN 0-89940-417-0

- Gordon, Kermit (ed.) *Agenda for the Nation,* the Brookings Institution. (1968)

- Lyndon B. Johnson My Hope for America: Random House, 1964   ISBN 1-121- 42877-0

- Sidney M. Milkis and Jerome M. Mileur, eds. *The Great Society And The High Tide Of Liberalism* (2005)

- Charles Murray Losing Ground: *American Social Policy, 1950-1980*: Basic Books; 10th Anniversary edition (February 1995) ISBN 0-465-04231-7

- Irwin Unger *The Best of Intentions: the triumphs and failures of the Great Society under Kennedy, Johnson, and Nixon:* Doubleday, 1996 ISBN 0-385- 46833-4

Chapter 16

The 10th Amendment

States Rights under the Constitution

Turning Points

The Fifty States have relinquished their rights and the rights of the people they represent.

Ratified in 1791 as part of the Bill of Rights:

The Tenth Amendment specifies that "the powers not delegated to the United States by the Constitution, nor prohibited by it to the States, are reserved to the States respectively, or to the people."

Of all the amendments demanded by anti-federalists in the state conventions that ratified the Constitution, one calling for a reserved powers clause was the most common. A number of Federalist spokesmen, including Alexander Hamilton, James Madison, and James Wilson, argued that no such clause was necessary. But fear of central authority was widespread and support for an explicit guarantee that the states should retain control over their internal affairs reached irresistible proportions. In response to these fears, James Madison, in *The Federalist* No. 45, maintained that the powers of a federal government are "few and defined" and extend "principally on external objects, as war, peace, negotiation, and foreign commerce," whereas the powers reserved to the states are "numerous and indefinite" and "extend to all objects which, in the ordinary course of affairs concern the lives, liberties, and properties of the people, and internal order, improvement, and prosperity of the State." In The Federalist No. 46, Madison reiterated the separation of powers doctrine by stating that the "Federal and State Governments are in fact but different agents and trustees of the people, instituted with different powers, and designated for different purposes." Few Federalists thought the amendment would be harmful, and thus it came as no surprise when Madison included a reserved powers clause among the amendments, he proposed in 1789.

Thomas Jefferson described the Tenth Amendment as "the foundation of the Constitution" and added, "To take a single step beyond the boundaries thus specially drawn … is to take possession of a boundless field of power, no longer susceptible of any definition." Jefferson's formulation of this doctrine of "strict construction" was echoed by champions of state sovereignty for many decades. The opposite, "loose construction" point of view, formulated by Secretary of the Treasury Hamilton, became the model for advocates of extended congressional power; but Hamilton's opinion did not conflict with the substance of the Tenth Amendment. Indeed, to him the Reserved Powers Clause was tautological, expressing a principle that inheres in any republican government. Since Hamilton specifically rejected any claim that Congress could interfere in the internal affairs of a state such concerns as the governance of the health, morality, education, and welfare of the people his stand was not an argument against the Tenth Amendment, but against its necessity.

Early pronouncements on the subject by the Supreme Court adhered to the proposition that the police power had been reserved exclusively to the states. Even Chief Justice John Marshall, whose decision upholding the constitutionality of the Second Bank of the United States in *McCulloch v. Maryland* (1819) closely reflected the reasoning in Hamilton's 1791 opinion, vehemently denied afterward that he had thereby contributed to "any extension by construction of the powers of Congress" and insisted that he had ruled upon the legitimacy of the "means" of carrying out a power that had been constitutionally delegated.

Thus, from the presidency of Jefferson to that of Abraham Lincoln, the consensus was that Jefferson had been right in calling the Tenth Amendment the foundation of the constitutional union. Indeed, at one time or another, state governments in all parts of the country defied the authority of the national government. New Englanders threatened secession after the Louisiana Purchase (1803) and again during the War of 1812 and blocked federal action during the Mexican War (1846–1848). Illinois, Ohio, and Wisconsin thwarted federal laws on several occasions. Southern states attempted to prevent the enforcement of federal laws in 1799 and the 1830s, and then in 1860–1861 eleven of them seceded. Everything changed temporarily during the Civil War and the Reconstruction that followed. The powers of the federal government were enormously increased during the war, and though there was considerable shrinkage afterward, the government never returned to its minuscule prewar proportions. Accordingly, the Tenth Amendment was virtually suspended for several years after the war, as far as the defeated and discredited southern states were concerned. Through armies of occupation, Congress governed those states directly, and the congressionally created Freedmen's Bureaus exercised the full range of police powers in regard to the former slaves. Of greater long-range significance, the Fourteenth Amendment opened the door for congressional action in areas that would earlier have been regarded as reserved to the states.

Nonetheless, the constitutional revolution was transitory. In 1883, the Supreme Court, having already limited the Fourteenth Amendment's protections of the rights of freedmen, declared the Civil Rights Act of 1875 unconstitutional on the ground that it was "repugnant to the Tenth Amendment" (*Civil Rights Cases*, p. During the next generation, the Court struck down a number of state exercises of the police power in keeping with the Tenth Amendment's "prohibited by it to the states" clause yet it never once allowed Congress to exercise a police power itself.

Erosion of the Tenth Amendment began early in the twentieth century. In 1895 Congress passed an act forbidding the shipment of lottery tickets in interstate commerce. The purpose was only nominally a regulation of commerce: its real purpose was to restrict gambling, a matter that had always been the exclusive domain of the states. In *Champion v. Ames* (1903), the Supreme Court upheld the act. The next year, the Court in *McCray* v. United States upheld a congressional act imposing a prohibitive excise tax on oleomargarine, which amounted to an exercise of a police power to protect the health of the citizenry, under the guise of a constitutional exercise of the power to levy taxes for the "general welfare." The Supreme Court was not, however, consistent in its rulings, and the justices were sorely, even angrily, divided during the next three decades. The tension, throughout the period, was between the Tenth Amendment on one side and the powers of Congress to regulate interstate commerce and to levy taxes on the other. The most important police power actions justified under the Commerce Clause were the Pure Food and Drug Act (1906), the Meat Inspection Acts (1906 and 1907), and the White Slave Traffic Act (1910); the Supreme Court upheld all of these, even though it had ruled in *Keller v. United States* (1909) that an act protecting women from immoral trafficking was an unconstitutional violation of the Tenth Amendment. The most important police power actions justified under the taxing power were the Phosphorous Match Act (1912) and the Harrison Anti-Narcotics Act (1914), both of which were approved by the Supreme Court despite arguments that they violated the Tenth Amendment.

Then in 1918, the Court dropped a bombshell. Congress, in keeping with the reform spirit of the times, had in 1916 passed an act prohibiting the shipment in interstate commerce of the products of mines or factories that employed children under the age of fourteen. Two years later, in *Hammer v. Dagenhart*, the Court ruled that the act was unconstitutional. In the majority opinion, Justice William R. Day inserted the word "expressly" into the Tenth: "It must never be forgotten that the nation is made up of states, to which are entrusted the powers of local government. And to them and to the people the powers that are not expressly delegated to the national government are reserved" (p. 275). The next year the Court upheld a prohibitive tax on the use of narcotics, but in *Bailey v. Drexel Furniture Company*

(1922) it held unconstitutional a second child labor law based upon the government's taxing power. In sum, the Supreme Court was sending mixed and confused signals to the Congress.

A new complication soon arose. Congress began to vote grants-in-aid to the states for various purposes, ranging from the prevention of forest fires to providing medical care for expectant mothers. In 1923 one such grant was challenged on the ground that it undermined the Tenth Amendment. In *Massachusetts v. Mellon* (1923) the Court rejected the argument, declaring that "the statute imposes no obligation, but simply extends an option which the state is free to accept or reject" (p. 480). Ultimately, and especially from the 1950s onward, grants-in-aid or "revenue sharing" would grow so large as to make the states, in many ways, mere appendages of federal administrative agencies.

In the meantime, the whole subject had come to a head and the Tenth Amendment was becoming a nullity in the wake of the Great Depression and World War II. Between 1934 and 1935, the Supreme Court declared unconstitutional a number of emergency economic recovery measures that formed part of Franklin Roosevelt's New Deal program. Among the most far-reaching was the National Industrial Recovery Act, which had authorized the president to negotiate with industry to draw up "codes of fair practices" that would have the force of law. Writing for a unanimous Court in *Schechter Poultry Corp.* v. United States (1935), Chief Justice Charles Evans Hughes gave three reasons for striking down the law, the first being that it flew directly in the face of the Tenth Amendment. However, the Court underwent drastic changes when a majority of the justices became Roosevelt appointees, thus sparking a constitutional revolution in 1937. It came as no surprise, then, that the Court in *Mulford v. Smith* (1939) completely rejected the Tenth Amendment opinions it had laid down in the child labor cases. In United States v. *Darby Lumber Co.* (1941), Chief Justice Harlan Fiske Stone reduced the amendment to nothing more than atriums, describing it as merely declaratory of intergovernmental relationships and as having no substantive meaning.

If the Tenth Amendment was ever a truism that changed commencing with Justice William H. Rehnquist's sole dissent in Fry v. United States (1975). Only a year later, in *National League of Cities v. Usery*, the Court held that application of the Fair Labor Standards Act to state and local government employees was a violation of the amendment. That decision opened so many problems, however, that the Court found it expedient to reverse itself explicitly in *Garcia v. San Antonio Metropolitan Transit Authority* (1985) when Justice Harry A. Blackmun unexpectedly switched his vote. In New York v. United States (1992), the Court reasoned that monetary and access incentives offered to the states to comply with the Low-Level Radioactive Waste Policy Amendments Act of 1985 was a valid exercise of Congress's power; the third incentive offered state governments a choice to accept ownership of waste or to follow the regulations of the 1985 act. According to the Court, by enacting this last provision, also known as "take-title" provision, Congress crossed the line that distinguishes encouragement from coercion. Similarly, in *Printz v. United States* (1997), the Court held that Congress may not issue "directives requiring the States to address particular problems, nor command the States' officers … to administer or enforce a federal regulatory program." More recently, in Reno v. Condon (2000), the Court held that Driver's Privacy Protection Act (1994) did not violate federalism principles as specified in New York v. United States and Printz v. United States; since unauthorized disclosure of a driver's personal information is a "thing in interstate commerce," it constitutes a proper subject of congressional regulation.

The conflict surrounding interpretation of the Tenth Amendment will inevitably continue to be a hot topic before the Supreme Court justices, for in as much as the states continue to exist as distinct political and legal entities and the Tenth Amendment remains a part of the Constitution, the tensions arising from dual and divided sovereignty remain.

Calhoun:

Most famous for his role in the pre-Civil War debate over states' rights, John Caldwell Calhoun was a U.S. senator from South Carolina (1832-43, 1845-50) and vice president under presidents John Quincy Adams (1825-29) and Andrew Jackson (1829-32). Calhoun grew up in South Carolina and was educated at Yale University before opening a law practice back home in Abbeville, South Carolina. He was a state representative (1808) and a U.S. representative (1811-1817) before serving as President Monroe's Secretary of War (1817-25). His terms as vice president were marked by his vocal differences with his presidents. Adams was an avid abolitionist from Boston, but Calhoun was a pro-slavery southern plantation owner, and Jackson and Calhoun were openly hostile to each other. Things heated up in the early 1830s over the issue of federal tariffs: Calhoun claimed that states could nullify federal laws, earning him the nickname of "Arch Nullifier," and Jackson threatened to use the army if South Carolina forced the issue. (Calhoun's colleague, Senator Henry Clay, helped work out a compromise.) Calhoun resigned as Jackson's vice president in 1832 and became a U.S. senator, then briefly served as Secretary of State under President Tyler (1844-45) and finally served in the Senate again until his death in 1850. After his death Calhoun became a symbol for southern unity and his likeness was used on the currency of the Confederate States of America during the Civil War (on $1000 bills in 1861 and $100 bills in 1862).

Calhoun, Clay and Daniel Webster, colleagues in the Senate, were dubbed the "Great Triumvirate" for their oratory and statesmanship... Calhoun was sometimes known as "the cast-iron man" for his cool logic and stern temperament... In 1959 a Senate committee named Calhoun one of the Senate's five most outstanding members ever (the committee was chaired by Senator John F. Kennedy of Massachusetts).

In the Twentieth Century:

Although the Union victory in the Civil War definitively ended the possibility of nullification and secession, the states' rights doctrine did not die. In the second half of the 20th century it was vigorously revived by Southern opponents of the federal civil-rights program. In the presidential election of 1948, a Southern states' rights party (the Dixiecrats) was organized with J. Strom Thurmond of South Carolina as its candidate, and it carried four Southern states. The desegregation controversy of the 1950s, 60s, and 70s engendered many states' rights statements by Southern political leaders such as Gov. George C. Wallace of Alabama. In 1962, federal troops were used at the Univ. of Mississippi to enforce a federal court ruling that ordered the admission of a black student to the university. Although the doctrine of states' rights is usually associated with the Southern wing of the Democratic Party, it is not exclusive to any particular section or political party. The vast increase in the powers of the federal government at the expense of the states, resulting from the incapacity of the states to deal with the complex problems of modern industrial civilization, has led to renewed interest in states' rights. In the 1980s and 90s, states' rights proponents, under the banner of "federalism" or "the New Federalism," attacked the great increase in federal government powers that had occurred since the New Deal. On taking power of both houses of Congress in the 1994 elections, conservative Republicans proclaimed the beginning of a process of "devolution," with much power reverting to the states; several years later, however, it was clear that reality had not met this prediction. State sovereignty has been affirmed and expanded, however, by recent, often narrowly decided, decisions of the Supreme Court.

Chapter 17

Arizona Stands for 10th Amendment Rights The Year 2010
The Tenth Amendment

Turning Points

The 10th Amendment

"The powers not delegated to the United States by the Constitution, nor prohibited by it to the states, are reserved to the states respectively, or to the people."

I find it hard to believe that the Supreme Court has had such a hard time in the interpretation of the 10th Amendment. It is clear cut without bias and there is no room for interpretation. It is what it is. Set aside your feelings and political views, that was not the point.

We had a *turning point* in the interpretation and when the states lost their rights and became under the US Government control by the Congress. The government took control of the money and how it is distributed to the states. The government will always dictate and mandate to each state how the money will be spent. However, that money does not continue after their mandate. It will be up to the states to raise taxes to ensure that the same amount of money will be available in future budgets. This is tyranny by our Federal Government.

Those states that are interested in sovereignty mandated by the Constitution, should declare their sovereignty and mandate to the Federal Government. When they take their rights back and the Federal

Government does not like that, then this states will succeed from the Union.

Should states start calling for sovereignty and some are, then the Federal Government will have to take notice. Many of them are plenty capable of sustaining without the power and control of the Federal Government. What would happen to the Federal Government? They would lose the revenue of each state and the control of the people. The federal government would be in turmoil and confusion. For the first time they would be rudderless.

"The Government serves best when it is afraid of the people but, when the people are afraid of the Government, the government will control and dictate, create more laws, more regulations more spending, all for the purpose of controlling the people. This is tyranny! That, my friend, is where we are! We as a people of this Great Nation need not fear the government but take control of it. It is our right under the Constitution and the Bill of Rights. Stand up for your rights for time is running out!"

Encourage your state leaders to stand on these principles and when they do, the federal government will get out of the way and out of your life, my life and our children and grand children's lives will become better and more fulfilled.

The less the federal government is involved in our lives the more creativity will occur. Government intervention will only stifle invention, prosperity and creativity. Government will never be the answer! It will always be the problem. Just look at all the other countries across the waters.

Our government is out of control!

They (Congress) benefits need to be cut off forever! We did not elect them to serve at their pleasure and we did not intend for them to retire on our dime! The President is one thing, but the Congress need to look at their expenses and the cost they have burdened the American people to pay for. The American people need to take a stand and make the change. We can do it! Shut down the congressional health plan, life insurance, etc. and make them pay for all their expenses. They have voted in pay raise after pay raise, more money for their office staff and their benefits. When will it stop! It will be up to us to make it stop.

When we do, they will crawl down the path to the sewer where they belong.

They are only looking out for themselves!

Their quote every day when they open the halls of congress has to be this?

"How much money and taxes do we need to demand from the entire fly over states?" We can raise more taxes and benefits for us and the uninsured. We can create more social programs, pass more laws that will indirectly and directly raise their tax burden and they will never know."

They think that we will pay because we are subjected to them!?

Well, I am not sorry; "We are in a battle for our country and our way of life!"

If we do not stand up during at this time then we never will, because there will never be another! This country will be lost!

The time has come!

Where do you stand? It may be your last!

As Arizona watches the demises of their land, state and sovereignty, the Federal Government does nothing; they have taken little to no action to protect theirs.

Chapter 18

Ronald Reagan

An Actor from California Ronald Reagan

Turning point to relieve the misguided in Government

A time for Choosing (aka "The Speech")

Air date 27 October 1964

Turning Points

Program Announcer: Ladies and gentlemen, we take pride in presenting a thoughtful address by Ronald Reagan. Mr. Reagan:

Reagan: Thank you. Thank you very much. Thank you and good evening. The sponsor has been identified, but unlike most television programs, the performer hasn't been provided with a script. As a matter of fact, I have been permitted to choose my own words and discuss my own ideas regarding the choice that we face in the next few weeks.

I have spent most of my life as a Democrat. I recently have seen fit to follow another course. I believe that the issues confronting us cross party lines. Now, one side in this campaign has been telling us that the issues of this election are the maintenance of peace and prosperity. The line has been used, "We've never had it so good."

But I have an uncomfortable feeling that this prosperity isn't something on which we can base our hopes for the future. No nation in history has ever survived a tax burden that reached a third of its national income. Today, 37 cents out of every dollar earned in this country is the tax collector's share, and yet our government continues to spend 17 million dollars a day more than the government takes in.

We haven't balanced our budget 28 out of the last 34 years. We've raised our debt limit three times in the last twelve months, and now our national debt is one and a half times bigger than all the combined debts of all the nations of the world. We have 15 billion dollars in gold in our treasury; we don't own an ounce. Foreign dollar claims are 27.3 billion dollars. And we've just had announced that the dollar of 1939 will now purchase 45 cents in its total value.

As for the peace that we would preserve, I wonder who among us would like to approach the wife or mother whose husband or son has died in South Vietnam and ask them if they think this is a peace that should be maintained indefinitely. Do they mean peace, or do they mean we just want to be left in peace? There can be no real peace while one American is dying some place in the world for the rest of us. We're at war with the most dangerous enemy that has ever faced mankind in his long climb from the swamp to the stars, and it's been said if we lose that war, and in so doing lose this way of freedom of ours, history will record with the greatest astonishment that those who had the most to lose did the least to prevent its happening. Well, I think it's time we ask ourselves if we still know the freedoms that were intended for us by the Founding Fathers.

Not too long ago, two friends of mine were talking to a Cuban refugee, a businessman who had escaped from Castro, and in the midst of his story one of my friends turned to the other and said, "We don't know how lucky we are." And the Cuban stopped and said, "How lucky you are? I had someplace to escape to." And in that sentence, he told us the entire story. If we lose freedom here, there's no place to escape to. This is the last stand on earth.

And this idea that government is beholden to the people, that it has no other source of power except the sovereign people, is still the newest and the most unique idea in all the long history of man's relation to man.

This is the issue of this election: whether we believe in our capacity for self- government or whether we abandon the American Revolution and confess that a little intellectual elite in a far-distant capitol can plan our lives for us better than we can plan them ourselves.

You and I are told increasingly we have to choose between a left or right. Well, I'd like to suggest there is no such thing as a left or right. There's only an up or down: [up] man's old old-aged dream, the ultimate in individual freedom consistent with law and order, or down to the ant heap of totalitarianism. And regardless of their sincerity, their humanitarian motives, those who would trade our freedom for security have embarked on this downward course.

In this vote-harvesting time, they use terms like the "Great Society," or as we were told a few days ago by the President, we must accept a greater government activity in the affairs of the people. But they've been a little more explicit in the past and among themselves; and all of the things I now will quote have appeared in print. These are not Republican accusations. For example, they have voices that say, "The cold war will end through our acceptance of a not undemocratic socialism." Another voice says, "The profit motive has become outmoded. It must be replaced by the incentives of the welfare state." Or, "Our traditional system of individual freedom is incapable of solving the complex problems of the 20th century." Senator Fulbright has said at Stanford University that the Constitution is outmoded. He referred to the President as "our moral teacher and our leader," and he says he is "hobbled in his task by the restrictions of power imposed on him by this antiquated document." He must "be freed," so that he "can do for us" what he knows "is best." And Senator Clark of Pennsylvania, another articulate spokesman, defines liberalism as "meeting the material needs of the masses through the full power of centralized government."

Well, I, for one, resent it when a representative of the people refers to you and me, the free men and women of this country, as "the masses." This is a term we haven't applied to ourselves in America. But beyond that, "the full power of centralized government" this was the very thing the Founding Fathers sought to minimize. They knew that governments don't control things. A government can't control the economy without controlling people. And they know when a government sets out to do that; it must use force and coercion to achieve its purpose. They also knew, those Founding Fathers, that outside of its legitimate functions, government does nothing as well or as economically as the private sector of the economy.

Now, we have no better example of this than government's involvement in the farm economy over the last 30 years. Since 1955, the cost of this program has nearly doubled. One-fourth of farming in America is responsible for 85% of the farm surplus. Three-fourths of farming is out on the free market and has known a

21% increase in the per capita consumption of all its produce. You see, that one- fourth of farming that's regulated and controlled by the federal government. In the last three years we've spent 43 dollars in the feed grain program for every dollar bushel of corn we don't grow.

Senator Humphrey last week charged that Barry Goldwater, as President, would seek to eliminate farmers. He should do his homework a little better, because he'll find out that we've had a decline of 5 million in the farm population under these government programs. He'll also find that the Democratic administration has sought to get from Congress [an] extension of the farm program to include three-fourths that is now free. He'll find that they've also asked for the right to imprison farmers who wouldn't keep books as prescribed by the federal government. The Secretary of Agriculture asked for the right to seize farms through condemnation and resell them to other individuals. And contained in that same program was a provision that would have allowed the federal government to remove 2 million farmers from the soil.

At the same time, there's been an increase in the Department of Agriculture employees. There's no one for every 30 farms in the United

States, and still they can't tell us how 66 shiploads of grain headed for Austria disappeared without a trace and Billie Sol Estes never left shore.

Every responsible farmer and farm organization has repeatedly asked the government to free the farm economy, but how   who are farmers to know what's best for them? The wheat farmers voted against a wheat program. The government passed it anyway. Now the price of bread goes up; the price of wheat to the farmer goes down.

Meanwhile, back in the city, under urban renewal the assault on freedom carries on. Private property rights [are] so diluted that public interest is almost anything a few government planners decide it should be. In a program that takes from the needy and gives to the greedy, we see such spectacles as in Cleveland, Ohio, a million-and-a-half-dollar building completed only three years ago must be destroyed to make way for what government officials call a "more compatible use of the land." The President tells us he's now going to start building public housing units in the thousands, where heretofore we've only built them in the hundreds.

But FHA [Federal Housing Authority] and the Veterans Administration tell us they have 120,000 housing units they've taken back through mortgage foreclosure. For three decades, we've sought to solve the problems of unemployment through government planning, and the more the plans fail, the more the planner's plan.
The latest is the Area Redevelopment Agency.

They've just declared Rice County, Kansas, a depressed area. Rice County, Kansas, has two hundred oil wells, and the 14,000 people there have over 30 million dollars on deposit in personal savings in their banks. And when the government tells you you're depressed, lie down and be depressed.

We have so many people who can't see a fat man standing beside a thin one without coming to the conclusion the fat man got that way by taking advantage of the thin one. So they're going to solve all the problems of human misery through government and government planning. Well, now, if government planning and welfare had the answer   and they've had almost 30 years of it   shouldn't we expect government to read the score to us once in a while? Shouldn't they be telling us about the decline each year in the number of people needing help? The reduction in the need for public housing?

But the reverse is true. Each year the need grows greater; the program grows greater. We were told four years ago that 17 million people went to bed hungry each night. Well, that was probably true. They were all on a diet. But now we're told that 9.3 million families in this country are poverty-stricken on the basis of earning less than 3,000 dollars a year. Welfare spending [is] 10 times greater than in the dark depths of the Depression. We're spending 45 billion dollars on welfare. Now do a little arithmetic, and you'll find that if we divided the 45 billion dollars up equally among those 9 million poor families, we'd be able to give each family 4,600 dollars a year. And this added to their present income should eliminate poverty. Direct aid to the poor, however, is only running only about 600 dollars per family. It would seem that someplace there must be some overhead.

Now   so now we declare "war on poverty," or "You, too, can be a Bobby Baker." Now do they honestly expect us to believe that if we add 1 billion dollars to the 45 billion we're spending, one more program to the 30-odd we have   and remember, this new program doesn't replace any, it just duplicates existing programs   do they believe that poverty is suddenly going to disappear by magic? Well, in all fairness I should explain there is one part of the new program that isn't duplicated. This is the youth feature. We're now going to solve the dropout problem, juvenile delinquency, by reinstituting something like the old CCC camps [Civilian Conservation Corps], and we're going to put our young people in these camps. But again we do some arithmetic, and we find that we're going to spend each year just on room and board for each young person we help 4,700 dollars a year. We can send them to Harvard for 2,700! Course, don't get me wrong. I'm not suggesting Harvard is the answer to juvenile delinquency.

But seriously, what are we doing to those we seek to help? Not too long ago, a judge called me here in Los Angeles. He told me of a young woman who'd come before him for a divorce. She had six children, was pregnant with her seventh.

Under his questioning, she revealed her husband was a laborer earning 250 dollars a month. She wanted a divorce to get an 80 dollar raise. She's eligible for 330 dollars a month in the Aid to Dependent Children Program. She got the idea from two women in her neighborhood who'd already done that very thing.

Yet anytime you and I question the schemes of the do-gooders, we're denounced as being against their humanitarian goals. They say we're always "against" things -

- we're never "for" anything.

Well, the trouble with our liberal friends is not that they're ignorant; it's just that they know so much that isn't so.

Now we're for a provision that destitution should not follow unemployment by reason of old age, and to that end we've accepted Social Security as a step toward meeting the problem.

But we're against those entrusted with this program when they practice deception regarding its fiscal shortcomings, when they charge that any criticism of the program means that we want to end payments to those people who depend on them for a livelihood. They've called it "insurance" to us in a hundred million pieces of literature. But then they appeared before the Supreme Court and they testified it was a welfare program. They only use the term "insurance" to sell it to the people. And they said Social Security dues are a tax for the general use of the government, and the government has used that tax. There is no fund, because Robert Byers, the actuarial head, appeared before a congressional committee and admitted that Social Security as of this moment is 298 billion dollars in the hole. But he said there should be no cause for worry because as long as they have the power to tax, they could always take away from the people whatever they needed to bail them out of trouble. And they're doing just that.

A young man, 21 years of age, working at an average salary — his Social Security contribution would, in the open market, buy him an insurance policy that would guarantee 220 dollars a month at age 65. The government promises 127. He could live it up until he's 31 and then take out a policy that would pay more than Social Security. Now are we so lacking in business sense that we can't put this program on a sound basis, so that people who do require those payments will find they can get them when they're due — that the cupboard isn't bare?

Barry Goldwater thinks we can.

At the same time, can't we introduce voluntary features that would permit a citizen who can do better on his own to be excused upon presentation of evidence that he had made provision for the non-earning years? Should we not allow a widow with children to work, and not lose the benefits supposedly paid for by her deceased husband? Shouldn't you and I be allowed to declare who our beneficiaries will be under this program, which we cannot do? I think we're for telling our senior citizens that no one in this country should be denied medical care because of a lack of funds. But I think we're against forcing all citizens, regardless of need, into a compulsory government program, especially when we have such examples, as was announced last week, when France admitted that their Medicare program is now bankrupt. They've come to the end of the road.

In addition, was Barry Goldwater so irresponsible when he suggested that our government give up its program of deliberate, planned inflation, so that when you do get your Social Security pension, a dollar will buy a dollar's worth, and not 45 cents worth?

I think we're for an international organization, where the nations of the world can seek peace. But I think we're against subordinating American interests to an organization that has become so structurally unsound that today you can muster a two-thirds vote on the floor of the General

Assembly among nations that represent less than 10 percent of the world's population. I think we're against the hypocrisy of assailing our allies because here and there they cling to a colony, while we engage in a conspiracy of silence and never open our mouths about the millions of people enslaved in the Soviet colonies in the satellite nations.

I think we're for aiding our allies by sharing of our material blessings with those nations which share in our fundamental beliefs, but we're against doling out money government to government, creating bureaucracy, if not socialism, all over the world. We set out to help 19 countries. We're helping 107. We've spent 146 billion dollars. With that money, we bought a 2 million dollar yacht for Haile Selassie. We bought dress suits for Greek undertakers, extra wives for Kenya[n] government officials. We bought a thousand TV sets for a place where they have no electricity. In the last six years, 52 nations have bought 7 billion dollars worth of our gold, and all 52 are receiving foreign aid from this country.

No government ever voluntarily reduces itself in size. So, governments' programs, once launched, never disappear.

Actually, a government bureau is the nearest thing to eternal life we'll ever see on this earth.

Federal employees   federal employees number two and a half million; and federal, state, and local, one out of six of the nation's work force employed by government. These proliferating bureaus with their thousands of regulations have cost us many of our constitutional safeguards. How many of us realize that today federal agents can invade a man's property without a warrant? They can impose a fine without a formal hearing, let alone a trial by jury? And they can seize and sell his property at auction to enforce the payment of that fine. In Chico County, Arkansas, James Wier over-planted his rice allotment. The government obtained a 17,000 dollar judgment. And a U.S. marshal sold his 960-acre farm at auction. The government said it was necessary as a warning to others to make the system work.

Last February 19th at the University of Minnesota, Norman Thomas, six-time candidate for President on the Socialist Party ticket, said, "If Barry Goldwater became President, he would stop the advance of socialism in the United States." I think that's exactly what he will do.

But as a former Democrat, I can tell you Norman Thomas isn't the only man who has drawn this parallel to socialism with the present administration, because back in 1936, Mr. Democrat himself, Al Smith, the great American, came before the American people and charged that the leadership of his Party was taking the Party of Jefferson, Jackson, and Cleveland down the road under the banners of Marx, Lenin, and Stalin. And he walked away from his Party, and he never returned till the day he died   because to this day, the leadership of that Party has been taking that Party, that honorable Party, down the road in the image of the labor Socialist Party of England.

Now it doesn't require expropriation or confiscation of private property or business to impose socialism on a people. What does it mean whether you hold the deed to the   or the title to your business or property if the government holds the power of life and death over that business or property? And such machinery already exists. The government can find some charge to bring against any concern it chooses to prosecute. Every businessman has his own tale of harassment.

Somewhere a perversion has taken place. Our natural, unalienable rights are now considered to be a dispensation of government, and freedom has never been so fragile, so close to slipping from our grasp as it is at this moment.

Our Democratic opponents seem unwilling to debate these issues. They want to make you and I believe that this is a contest between two men   that we're to choose just between two personalities.

Well, what of this man that they would destroy   and in destroying, they would destroy that which he represents, the ideas that you and I hold dear? Is he the brash and shallow and trigger-happy man they say he is? Well, I've been privileged to know him "when." I knew him long before he ever dreamed of trying for high office, and I can tell you personally I've never known a man in my life I believed so incapable of doing a dishonest or dishonorable thing.

This is a man who, in his own business before he entered politics, instituted a profit-sharing plan before unions had ever thought of it. He put in health and medical insurance for all his employees. He took 50 percent of the profits before taxes and set up a retirement program, a pension plan for all his employees. He sent monthly checks for life to an employee who was ill and couldn't work. He provides nursing care for the children of mothers who work in the stores. When Mexico was ravaged by the floods in the Rio Grande, he climbed in his airplane and flew medicine and supplies down there.

An ex-GI told me how he met him. It was the week before Christmas during the Korean War, and he was at the Los Angeles airport trying to get a ride home to Arizona for Christmas. And he said that [there were] a lot of servicemen there and no seats available on the planes. And then a voice came over the loudspeaker and said, "Any men in uniform wanting a ride to Arizona, go to runway such-and- such," and they went down there, and there was a fellow named Barry Goldwater sitting in his plane. Every day in those weeks before Christmas, all day long, he'd load up the plane, fly it to Arizona, fly them to their homes, fly back over to get another load.

During the hectic split-second timing of a campaign, this is a man who took time out to sit beside an old friend who was dying of cancer. His campaign managers were understandably impatient, but he said, "There aren't many left who care what happens to her. I'd like her to know I care." This is a man who said to his 19- year-old son, "There is no foundation like the rock of honesty and fairness, and when you begin to build your life on that rock, with the cement of the faith in God that you have, and then you have a real start." This is not a man who could carelessly send other people's sons to war. And that is the issue of this campaign that makes all the other problems I've discussed academic, unless we realize we're in a war that must be won.

Those who would trade our freedom for the soup kitchen of the welfare state have told us they have a utopian solution of peace without victory. They call their policy "accommodation." And they say if we'll only avoid any direct confrontation with the enemy, he'll forget his evil ways and learn to love us. All who oppose them are indicted as warmongers. They say we offer simple answers to complex problems. Well, perhaps there is a simple answer not an easy answer but simple: If you and I have the courage to tell our elected officials that we want our national policy based on what we know in our hearts is morally right.

We cannot buy our security, our freedom from the threat of the bomb by committing an immorality so great as saying to a billion human beings now enslaved behind the Iron Curtain, "Give up your dreams of freedom because to save our own skins, we're willing to make a deal with your slave masters." Alexander Hamilton said, "A nation which can prefer disgrace to danger is prepared for a master, and deserves one." Now let's set the record straight. There's no argument over the choice between peace and war, but there's only one guaranteed way you can have peace and you can have it in the next second surrender.

Admittedly, there's a risk in any course we follow other than this, but every lesson of history tells us that the greater risk lies in appeasement, and this is the specter our well-meaning liberal friends refuse to face that their policy of accommodation is appeasement, and it gives no choice between peace and war, only between fight or surrender. If we continue to accommodate, continue to back and retreat, eventually we have to face the final demand the ultimatum. And what then when

Nikita Khrushchev has told his people he knows what our answer will be? He has told them that we're retreating under the pressure of the Cold War, and someday when the time comes to deliver the final ultimatum, our surrender will be voluntary, because by that time we will have been weakened from within spiritually, morally, and economically. He believes this because from our side he's heard voices pleading for "peace at any price" or "better Red than dead," or as one commentator put it, he'd rather "live on his knees than die on his feet." And therein lays the road to war, because those voices don't speak for the rest of us.

You and I know and do not believe that life is so dear and peace so sweet as to be purchased at the price of chains and slavery. If nothing in life is worth dying for, when did this begin just in the face of this enemy? Or should Moses have told the children of Israel to live in slavery under the pharaohs? Should Christ have refused the cross? Should the patriots at Concord Bridge have thrown down their guns and refused to fire the shot heard 'round the world? The martyrs of history were not fools, and our honored dead who gave their lives to stop the advance of the Nazis didn't die in vain. Where, then, is the road to peace? Well, it's a simple answer after all.

You and I have the courage to say to our enemies, "There is a price we will not pay." "There is a point beyond which they must not advance." And this this is the meaning in the phrase of Barry Goldwater's "peace through strength." Winston Churchill said, "The destiny of man is not measured by material computations. When great forces are on the move in the world, we learn we're spirits not animals." And he said, "There's something going on in time and space, and beyond time and space, which, whether we like it or not, spells duty."

You and I have a rendezvous with destiny.

We'll preserve for our children this, the last best hope of man on earth, or we'll sentence them to take the last step into a thousand years of darkness.

We will keep in mind and remember that Barry Goldwater has faith in us. He has faith that you and I have the ability and the dignity and the right to make our own decisions and determine our own destiny.

Thank you very much.

Chapter 19

The Carter Years

More Social Programs

Another Turning Point in American history:

Turning Points

As Governor of Georgia:

In his inaugural address Carter announced his intentions to aid all poor and needy Georgians, regardless of race. This speech won Carter his first national attention, for in it he called for an end to racial discrimination and the extension of a right to an education, to a job, and to "simple justice" for the poor. As governor, Carter worked for, and signed into law, a bill which stipulated that the poor and wealthy areas of Georgia would have equal state aid for education.

Before I continue, President Carter served 7 years as a naval officer. At least he served. I salute his service.

That being said:

Back to his social programs.

Carter's domestic policies for the United States were those of Georgia at large. He promoted civil rights, welfare, tax reform, and budgetary control. Almost immediately, however, two major domestic concerns began to dictate his agenda. One was the nation's energy supply. In the late 1970s a severe energy crisis produced the worst fuel shortage in U.S. history coupled with rising international prices for oil. Congress cooperated with Carter's remedies by approving fuel conservation policies, deregulating natural gas prices, and passing a windfall tax on oil company profits. He did not get everything he wanted: a federal court blocked his attempt to decontrol domestic oil prices and Congress denied him authority for gasoline rationing. The second major problem was the economy, which worsened over the course of his term. His effort to fight inflation especially controls on consumer credit produced a recession. Voters grew disgruntled. His approval rating fell and a July 1979 speech in which he blamed the nation's problems on a spiritual "malaise" was disastrous: afterward, a *v* poll showed that for the first time ever, U.S. citizens, who traditionally had responded 2-1 that they were optimistic about the future, now said nearly 2- 1 that they were pessimistic. (Answers.com).

President Carter has been tagged as the worst President in American history, until the current President, President Barack Obama took office.

Chapter 20

Are they pouring Gas on the Coals of Liberty?

Turning Point towards Liberalism and Progressivism

Turning Points

The coals of Liberty first received a glimmer of heat burning in their hearts as the campaign for president of the United States moved quickly towards the election in 2009. As the rhetoric continued during the campaign it became more apparent the peoples Liberty was being challenged. It was as if the people could see a flicker in the coals and through that flicker was a light. The election came and their hearts stopped for they knew dark times would be coming and the light dimmed.

They could see over the horizon for America and for their future, their children, grandchildren and maybe countless generations, based on campaign rhetoric, that their way of life was being threatened and the flicker became diminished and the coals lay quite in the night.

Was it the light that drove them forward or was it the flicker of a flame for Liberty in their hearts?

Liberty was still burning and the power of the government was inevitably continuing its growth and the people were still sitting on the side lines watching the destruction of Liberty and their Republic being destroyed right before their eyes.

The flicker was still in their hearts and the light was spreading across their neighborhoods and into the networks across America on April 15, 2009.

It was as if the American people had finally felt the heat that has been spewing from the federal government for generations. The reason was this was the time for those that knew what Liberty was to get off the couch and take to the streets. They could see that their voices were not being heard and they must do something.

The coals were lying dormant and smoldering and with a deep breath the people did something most would have never done. They poured a little patriotism (gas) on the coals and with one fail breath blew into the smoldering coal and breathed life into Liberty and the Republic. They created a movement that reached across party lines, across races and into the living rooms of all Americans. They knew their time had come!

They had their meetings, said a prayer, to their God, and pledged to their flag! They went forth into the streets and into the bawls of town hall meetings.

They marched with their friends and family to local, county, state and federal governments.

They took their time and money and marched on government. With all their efforts their voices were falling on deaf ears. They continued to see the wrath of the Almighty Government come crashing down around them as more deficits, entitlements, bailouts and mandates formed a circle around their Republic. Even with all that, they could fell the shocking of their voice! For some reason, their voice was unheard, so they moved forward, like Christian Soldiers, into the battle.

The coals of Liberty and Justice continued to grow and the flame (people) was growing brighter as many that had opposed them were know seeing the light and the misgivings of their deed's. Those that apposed them were falling to the side and realizing what they did was wrong and more and more of them joined the fight!

It appears that the more the government tries to take away from the people; they are only pouring more GAS on the coals (Patriots and true Americas).

Chapter 21

Is the elevator to the President's office out of order?

Did the American People get the Change they wanted?

Turning Points

Since the campaign and the election in 2008 and all the rhetoric that inspired a nation to elect him, did it transform into something that was not expected? Yes, his campaign was about change and all his followers wanted change, but did they really know the man and the kind of change he would pursue?

He had a history and a trail of advisers, church leaders and others over his life that should have given a RED FLAG to all his followers and those that did not vote for him, that something was just not right. But, the misinformed public took the bait, just as a fish out of water would do looking for water and a chance to breath.

However, the bait was swallowed by the misinformed and the hook was set. They all fell into his waters and took the breath and the reality was soon to follow.

The change was coming and it was coming with a vengeance.

He has shown no regard for the Constitution. He has even stated that he thinks it is an out lived out dated document and is a burden and interferes with government. He has bowed to more enemies of the United States than any other head of state and/or President in history.

He has stated we are not a Christian nation founded on Christian principles. Did one RED FLAG show up!

Over the last year the people have seen more, he has taken over two auto companies, insurance companies, financial companies, student aid, has more czars than any president, the first lady has over 100 people waiting on her hand and foot, (first in history) and he has been on the TV, radio and everywhere every day since he took his oath as president. It is as if the campaign is still in full swing and the election never happened.

Many Americans across this great land saw something that was disarming. They could see a government that is leading the people down a path of destruction and our civil liberties, our Constitution and Bill of Rights. They could see the states being more burdened with un-mandated tax increase and the people would be the only ones to pay and the PEOPLE stood up, got off the couch and took to the streets.

Over the horizons, driven with passion and faith, the people looked for a path to the oval office. They could see the elevator of the almighty BO and the congress but the elevator was out of order for the people. They had control and people meant nothing, so the people decided to take the next step.

The stairs were wide open. The Patriots and the T.E.A parties crawled off the couch and like true Patriots descended upon governments and candidates across the land. They decided to take the stairs, one step at a time. With each step they started vetting the candidates, attending town hall meetings, marching on local, state governments and they marched all the way to D.C. They made their voices heard in various elections and they decided that they would take each step with those that understood the Constitution of the United States.

The stair well is full with Patriots and Constitutional people and they are making a difference as each take a step up the stairs.

Chapter 22

Obama's Rules of Revolution/The New Killing Fields

The Law of Compelled Performance

By: Timothy Lamb

Turning Points

Only the hopelessly blind cannot see that America is rapidly falling into the iron grip of the communist forces that now occupy our domestic power base. The majority of American people, not understanding the nature of tyranny, are about to get a very rude awakening. Those brave souls that have had the backbone to resist and oppose this system of lawlessness will soon be demonized as if they are the enemy of the nation.

Look around and see if you see any lessons of history that are currently being replayed on a new and ignorant generation of people. Hitler had a plan which he utilized to neutralize his potential enemies and ultimately murder them without reservation.

1. He identified his target group as a public menace.

2. He confiscated the property of these unfortunate individuals.

3. He banished the targeted group to isolated locations.

4. He then annihilated the targeted group.

Our current government administration has begun the same process as seen in a new report recently put out by The School of Advanced Military Studies along with the assistance of The United States Army Command and General Staff College out of Fort Leavenworth, Kansas.

A brief overview of this report testifies to the fact that our current leaders in government consider Bible-believing Christians to be an enemy that must be marginalized, watched and controlled. Christians have been labeled as "Problematic" to U.S. Government policy objectives and are considered as adversaries. Military leaders are now planning action to mitigate the perceived threat Christians pose to the Obama communist regime.

The National Security Agencies surveillance project code named, "Main Core", lists all Americans considered to be "Potential Domestic Terrorists" or "Enemy Combatants of the State." These Americans are simply those that believe in Constitutional Law and limited government power.

Understanding the Law of Compelled Performance is essential to the realization of where we as Americans stand on the road to the total loss of freedom and liberty in our nation.

To begin with, it is useful to know that various titles of government have different names but all mean the same thing. The Law of Compelled Performance is also referred to as Kings Rule, The Law of Admiralty, Statutory Jurisdiction and the Law of the Sea. These various titles all mean the same thing; that you have no rights but only a few privileges that the government can suspend at any given time.

To give an example of law we will examine and explain that under the Constitutional authority of early America, a crime was defined as an act that destroyed the life, liberty or property of another individual. So for a crime to exist there had to be a damaged party. Under the Law of Compelled Performance a crime is defined as breaking any of the rules set forth by the governing authority. A simple example would be a traffic violation. If an individual is traveling 75 MPH in a 65 MPH speed zone, has the individual performing the act damaged anyone's life, liberty or property? No, but on the other hand, the rules set forth by the governing authority have been broken. No crime has actually been committed but punishment is based on the person's failure to comply with the king's rules.

The truth of the matter is that typical speeding violations have nothing to do with public safety but are in reality just revenue tools used by local municipalities to fund their bank accounts. The object of this discussion is not to debate the value of traffic laws but rather to show the progressive nature of the Law of Compelled Performance. The nature of compelled performance is that it always increases in its demands until the governed population refuses to comply.

Under the Law of Compelled Performance the governing body imposes its tax demand on the population until they must labor 20 hours a day to maintain any type of lifestyle under the tax burden. Under compelled performance the government determines that you will accept homosexuality as just another lifestyle which they will teach to your children as a good thing in the public education system. They will then compel you to accept gay marriage in each of the various states. Lately we have been compelled to accept a national health care system that will have Americans shouldering the financial burden of medical treatment for 25 million illegal aliens.

Coming soon will be the declaration that the American people must accept amnesty for these 25 million illegal aliens so the government can control all future election results, in reality, stealing any opportunity for the people to have any effective voice or control in their national affairs. The ultimate outcome of the Law of Compelled Performance is that the American people will be compelled to perform until the point that they resist and then they will be declared enemies of the state and be dealt with by the use of military force.

Under Constitutional Law, a person can only enter into a contract knowingly and willingly but under Admiralty Law a person can enter into a contract unknowingly by partaking of a privilege. The privilege that the American people accepted that entered them into the Law of Compelled Performance was the acceptance of the use of Federal Reserve Notes back in 1913. In the eyes of the law there is a big difference between discharging a debt with a fraudulent currency verses paying a debt with lawful money of substance. By accepting the privilege of using Federal Reserve Notes to discharge debt we unknowingly entered the system of compelled performance. In 1938 the courts of the land started the transition from Constitutional Law to that of Compelled Performance because once you accept a privilege you forfeit your rights as a nation.

This author has addressed the issues of monetary policy many times in the past so will not do so again at this particular time. Many Americans now understand the consequences of using paper money that the government can print without any restrictions. Hyper inflation, due to government printing presses, has ushered in every dictator in the history of the world. The total destruction of the value of the currency of a nation always leads to anarchy and the resulting police state.

Another main point of discussion that the American people need to understand is that tyranny always comes into its full potential with the aid of the nation's so- called spiritual leaders. Those manning the pulpits remain silent concerning the crimes of government against its own people. The people effectively remain ignorant as to the nature of tyranny until it is way too late for them to effectively resist. The benefit that has led our spiritual leaders to betray their own people and enter into their covenant of silence with the forces of evil is that of their tax exempt status. To retain the financial windfall that tax exemption provides, these frauds standing in our pulpits must agree to remain silent concerning the crimes of government.

Not all pastors are included in this indictment, there are many pastors in America that have not taken the bribe of exemption but the majority have and these are the ones that cannot be trusted when the chips are down. In Germany, when Hitler came into full control, it did not take any time at all for the majority of the German clergy to sign an oath of allegiance to the new dictator. The frauds that we have in our pulpits have already committed to Satan by their acceptance of tax exemption in return for their silence. To remain silent when one has the moral obligation to speak is nothing less than fraud.

The gutless preachers in this country have paved the road to the destruction of our Constitutional Republic by their ignorance and by their arrogance. Due to the indifference of these phony frauds posing as men of God, America now finds itself on the verge of becoming an oppressive and tyrannical state.

God's judgment on these traitors to the Christian faith and traitors to the nation is the blinding of their minds. They cannot now comprehend that their destruction is upon them. They do not understand that when the hammer of tyranny falls, it will be directly on top of their arrogant heads. The final assault is soon coming to America and when it strikes overnight, these sorry frauds will get their just punishment and there will be nothing that saves them from their destruction.

One final word of little known truth about most churches is that they are not really churches at all. Under the law of incorporation, once a church incorporates and accepts the gift of tax exemption, they forfeit their status as a church and become a non-profit state agency and the pastor becomes an agent of the state. When a person gets married under the law of the land, they can still insist that they are single but they are not, they are married once the legal act is completed. Churches can insist they are still churches after they incorporate but they are not. Once the incorporation process is complete they are agents of the state and the state controls the material presented from the pulpit. They can shout and say they love Jesus all they want but the truth of the matter is that whoever controls your mouth is your God. People, don't waste any more of your hard earned money on these fraudulent institutions because God does not honor fraud.

Common sense dictates that it is prudent to understand during the American Revolution the torch of liberty was carried by a very small percentage of the American population. The responsibility to defend freedom will once again fall upon the small minority who understand the true nature and tactics of tyranny in all of its forms. Those who recognize the enemy do so because they are looking for them while the vast majority remains ignorant and clueless concerning the peril that they are now in.

The iron fist of tyranny is always covered with a velvet glove until such time that they are ready to snap the trap on an unsuspecting population. The vast majority of men in America do not understand the nature of tyranny nor do they understand the reason that they should even own a weapon. These simple minded individuals will soon learn the lesson realized by the Russian people when communism took over their nation.

What the Russian people soon realized after the communists had captured the reins of power was that murder was to be the order of the day. When the communists began the middle of the night visits to the homes of their victims they dragged them out of their homes and put a bullet in their heads the first time that they came. The communists claimed that they were simply looking for guns that had been recently banned but as the Russian people soon learned it was not about guns. The communists executed these people whether or not they had weapons because it was not about guns; it was about the way the people thought.

Men and women of America, you have been raised under the American rule of law. You have been educated under a system of Constitutional Law and you are not re-trainable. You will be taken out and shot by the new masters of the universe because of the way you think. Early Americans understood a very simple concept of if you won't prepare to fight when victory is relatively easy with little cost of life, then there will come a time when you have to fight with no hope of victory because death is better than slavery. Thousands of

Russian farmers displayed this truth when they had suffered enough and charged multiple communist machine gun positions with only pitch forks as their weapons. They chose death over slavery, a choice that America will soon have to make itself.

A comment for the Christian community who are finally beginning to recognize the threat to their liberty and freedom, many of you have the false belief that this coming persecution is the result of some end time scenario rather than accept the fact that it is your own doing. The colonial pastors taught long ago that the noblest way of professing Christ to the world was by openly opposing the evil that floods over our land. The modern church in America, along with its congregations, has done nothing to oppose evil for the past 70 years. The people of the church, for the most part, have been absent from the battle field where war has been waged for the life of their nation. The coming persecution that you will now endure is because you have refused to be the salt that preserves liberty in America and you are now good for nothing but to be trampled under the feet of Godless men.

To the brave men and women that have been standing in the gap, the enemy is now inside the gate, unfortunately there's a man walking up the road with chains for you. Go back in your history books to research and remember the words of General George Washington and General George S. Patton. These men both made the comment that if you give me one hundred good men unafraid to die, I can destroy ten thousand of my enemy.

The Bible tells us that the wise see danger and prepare while the simple minded ignore the truth and keep going down their path to destruction. Those that have eyes to see and ears to hear, prepare to defend you. As in the days of our American Revolution, those who stand in the gap and oppose tyranny will be honored by God. At some point the Lord of Heaven will send angels to fight on our behalf if we stand firm and fulfill our Christian responsibility to duty and the defense of liberty.

For those who refuse to fulfill their duty to God and country here is a message for you from Samuel Adams that was made in 1776.

"If ye love wealth better than liberty, the tranquility of servitude better than the animating contest of freedom, go home from us in peace. We ask neither your counsel nor your arms. Crouch down and lick the hands which feed you. May your chains set lightly upon you, and may posterity forget that you were our countrymen."

As stated previously, our enemies have gotten inside the gate. The beast is not coming at some future date, the beast is here. America, prepare to stand strong and defend yourself.

It is a known fact that Hitler quoted Bible scripture to the German Christians to assure their submission to his tyranny. He used Roman's 13 to brow beat Christians over the head as if the Bible mandated their obedience to his murderous agenda. Unfortunately, American Christians, due to their ignorance of Biblical application could just as easily be hood winked by the current government authorities.

Christians need to realize that all authority delegated to men from God has very specific limits. Those in authority must govern by the use of justice and by proper law. They are not little despots that can just do as they please with immunity and without consequences.

Rev. Jonathan Mayhew, considered to be the father of civil and religious liberty in America, in 1750 expressed the point of view that: *"Those in authority may abuse their trust and power to such a degree that neither the law of reason nor of religion requires that any obedience or submission be paid to them; but on the contrary, that they should be totally discarded, and the authority which they were before vested with transferred to others, who may exercise more to those good purposes for which it is given."* Rev. Simeon Howard stated in 1773 that, *"For men to stand fast in their liberty means in general, resisting the attempts that are made against it, in the best and most effectual manner they can. When anyone's liberty is attacked or threatened, he is first to try gentle methods for his safety; to reason with and persuade the adversary to desist, if there be opportunity for it; or get out of his way if he can; and if by such means he can prevent the injury, he is to use no other. But, the experience of all ages has shown that those who are so unreasonable as to form designs of injuring others are seldom to be diverted from their purpose by argument and persuasion alone. When the attempts to inflict injury become of a capital nature, then a defensive posture is sometimes necessary, even to the point of the use of arms!"* The Rev. Howard also stated that, *"The first indication of a nation in moral decline is that of the men losing their martial spirit!"*

War is a horrible reality but there are things worse than war. Men that have no sense of responsibility to stand and fight for the cause of Christian liberty, for the freedom of their children, are by far much worse than the actual clash of war because to these men nothing is worth fighting for and they will sacrifice all liberty for peace in their time. The only reason that they are free is because of other men, better than themselves, having fought to preserve that privilege for them.

One early American authority in matters of law was Sir William Blackstone who once stated, *"No man or set of men can create law. Man has no power, no authority, and no jurisdiction to make law. He can and he is supposed to enforce and obey God's law. Civil servants have no delegated authority to legalize crime, make lawful acts illegal, or illegal acts lawful. Man must obey the Law! This means he must obey God! To obey men in violation of God's law would be the highest form of treason against God!"*

"When the Congress, state legislatures, or city governments pass ordinances that would confiscate a man's labor, rob his children of their inheritance, or redistribute the wealth to the lazy and wicked, and support abortion and sodomy, Godly men are compelled to refuse to comply with such ordinances. No man can serve two masters; either he will serve God or the state."

"Law is the embodiment of those powers created by God for the protection of life, liberty and property. When government ceases to fulfill the proper role of government, primarily the protection of life, liberty and property or even worse yet, when it becomes the force under the color of law to kill, imprison and steal from its citizens, then men not only may, but have a duty to alter, remove or destroy the persons or form of government which perpetrates such crimes against the citizenry!"

From the Sixteenth American Jurisprudence, Second Edition, Section 256: *"The general rule is that an unconstitutional statute, though having the form and name of law, is in reality no law, but is wholly void, and ineffective for any purpose; since unconstitutionality dates from the time of its enactment, and not merely from the date of the decision so branding it. An unconstitutional law, in legal contemplation, is as inoperative as if it had never been passed. Such a statute leaves the question it purports to settle just as it would be had the statute not been enacted."*

"Since an unconstitutional law is void, the general principles follow that it imposes no duties, confers no rights, creates no office, bestows no power or authority to anyone, affords no protection, and justifies no acts performed under it."

"A void act cannot be legally consistent with a valid one. An unconstitutional law cannot operate to supersede any existing valid law. Indeed, insofar as a statute runs counter to the fundamental law of the land, it is superseded thereby.

No one is bound to obey an unconstitutional law and no courts are bound to enforce it!"

Every member in Congress and the Senate of these United States of America knows that Obama is not a natural born citizen of this country and is totally ineligible for the office of President. He does not even qualify to be a boy scout. Obama is rapidly dismantling this constitutional republic without opposition because those in the halls of Congress and the Senate are for the most part communists as well. I sit behind closed doors with pastors and listen to them moan with fear for what they know is soon coming but they offer no voice of warning to the people in their congregations. Pastors in early America viewed themselves as watchmen upon the wall, to warn their people when danger was approaching. The cowards in our pulpits today feel no such responsibility. Today's institutional churches follow man and not God. They truly serve the forces of evil by their silence, and they have forfeited any useful purpose in our society. Underneath the shallow layer of modern Christian leadership is a heart of rebellion with no real desire for the ageless truths of the Bible or the things of God.

It is unfortunate that it has come to the point where our church leaders must be confronted with their pitiful spiritual condition; however, confrontation for the sake of truth is commanded by God. Surely, the majority of pastors in America have no business standing in a pulpit; they, for the most part, would be better suited as door greeters at the local Big Mart store.

Unfortunately, Americans have lost the ability to think and to discern that which is not obvious. They fail to see through subtle deception and cannot recognize the difference between good and evil. Non-thinking, non-discerning people who have forgotten their history will not understand the deteriorating political, financial situation in this country nor will they in any way oppose the decline. They hate bad news, and they hate the person who brings it!!!

As we continue to witness our nation being raped, pillaged and brutalized by the most traitorous group of government officials ever assembled, be comforted by the fact that millions of Americans are rapidly waking up to the reality of the situation and they are getting very angry. Michael Connelly recently issued a stern warning to the Obama Administration by stating, *"I have some bad news for all of the socialists in American government; you have made a huge mistake. Following the attack on Pearl Harbor, Japanese Admiral Yamamoto who led the attack said that, 'I fear all we have done is to awaken a sleeping giant and fill him with a terrible resolve."* Connelly continued in saying, *"I suggest to Obama, Pelosi and Reid that you have awakened the giant again and that this giant, made up of freedom loving Americans, is going to be coming at you from every direction you can imagine!"*

Writer J.D. Longstreet also issued a warning to the communist regime in Washington DC saying that, *"The American people are a patient people. We will put up with a lot of nonsense from our government – for a while. But we draw the line when that government ignores the Constitution, as the Obama Regime and the Democrats in the Congress have done. There is a seething rage in America today… my senses tell me it is too late to avoid the 'lashing out' that Americans are about to unleash. Americans are waiting, just waiting, for an incident that will knock the chocks from the dam wall holding back the cascade. Postponing, or suspending, the midterm election would be the spark that ignites a firestorm that will consume all in its path!"*

Police and military personnel that are still loyal to God and country have in recent weeks given valuable information concerning the various theaters of operation that will very soon be conducting their traitorous activities within our cities and towns.

Police sources have verified that several Adjutant Generals of National Guard units recently met with federal government agencies to determine their role in confiscating weapons from the American people. Also, U.N. troops are now being given permanent assignments in peace keeping units housed on U.S. military bases around the country. The government is developing a 'Special Force' in our National Guard and city police departments consisting of 'Special Officers.' They will do anything they are told to do! They're so special that they will put a .308

rifle slug through your head when ordered to do so. These are the types of ruthless men that have been brought into the system.

A few weeks ago federal agents conducted two gang summits, one in Kansas City and one in L.A. Thirty top gang leaders were brought together to discuss their duties which will consist of house to house search and seizure operations and gang violence across the nation in major cities to de-stabilize the country and instill fear in the hearts of the weak and timid.

The federal government has had a working relationship with gangs for years. The government has been bringing drugs into the country and using gangs to disperse the drugs. Professional undercover police investigators have verified this evidence and it is all true. The benefits of using gangs are listed as follows:

a) Regimentation – They have one leader that they will die for and he gives the orders.

b) They are battle hardened more than the military – they can be shot or stabbed and they will still fight.

c) They are ruthless and will do whatever they are told to do.

d) They will participate to keep the plunder they take from the population.

e) They are expendable – they don't know what is going to happen to them – they will be executed.

f) One final fact that few people realize, these gangs are not just bad guys randomly committing acts of violence – a large percent of gang members are radical Muslims on a mission to destroy America.

Two weeks ago a police alert came out verifying that 700 gang members had converged on the Country Plaza Mall in south central

Kansas City. Armed robberies were committed in daylight while many civilians were brutalized and terrorized. There gangs have received their operational orders from Washington DC and are doing their job as commanded.

Another formidable opponent of the American people will be an organization referred to as FICEN – Financial Crimes Enforcement Network. This is a U.N. group operating inside the U.S. made up mostly of Europeans, troops that are Belgians, French, Dutch and Germans. They are more ruthless than gang members. They are one of the fiercest fighting forces known in the world, second only to pissed off Americans. They are also mercenaries that will work for plunder. Their main mission statement will be to round up known dissidents and interrogate them.

The government has stated that these forces are to be used only against the criminal element of society. Unfortunately, thousands of Americans will become criminals at the stroke of a pen when they are told to surrender their weapons and they refuse to do so.

Let recent history be a warning to those that feel they can surrender their weapons with no consequences. In 1929, the Soviet Union confiscated the weapons of the Russian people then proceeded to murder 20 million dissidents that were unable to defend themselves. In 1911, the Turkish government disarmed their people then 1.5 million were rounded up and exterminated. Germany took the weapons from their people before World War II and slaughtered 13 million people consisting of Jews and many others that resisted the new tyranny. The communist government in China wiped out more than 65 million people once they were rendered helpless by not being allowed to own weapons. The list goes on and on, North Korea executed over 2 million. In Africa more than 2 million were put to death. Cambodia killed over 2 million of its own people; anyone that disagreed with the public policy of the state was hauled off and executed. The total number of defenseless people rounded up and exterminated by communist governments in the 20th Century has exceeded 100 million people.

It is interesting to note that the pioneers of American liberty believed the second amendment of the constitution is what actually guarantees our freedom. What else can ensure that the government will respect all of our other constitutional rights? After all, any constitutional right is nothing but words on a piece of paper. They have no power within themselves to force a government to comply with their terms. They believed that it is only the right of individuals to keep and bear arms that puts teeth into the Bill of Rights. It is that right which ensures that no future administration will be able to run roughshod over the rights of the people. It is that God-given right that forces a tyrannical government to count the cost of imposing itself upon us or our children. Clearly, in the minds of our Fathers, without the second amendment, all the others are mere paper tigers.

George Mason in the Virginia Constitutional Convention stated in 1788 that, *"Divine Providence has given to every individual the means of self-defense."* During the same convention Patrick Henry stated, *"The great object is that every man be armed…. Everyone who is able may have a gun."* The framers of the Bill of Rights used the term 'select militia' and applied the term as defining a 'universally armed people!'

The Declaration of Independence asserted that all men were *"Endowed by their Creator with certain unalienable Rights,"* and among these God-given rights was the right of self-defense. The Declaration stated that when a government is bent on usurping the rights of the people, *"It is their Right; it is their Duty, to throw off such a Government, and to provide new guards for their future security."*

U.S. Congressman Elbridge Gerry stated in 1787 that, *"Self defense is a primary law of nature, which no subsequent law of society can abolish; this* primeval principle, the immediate gift of the Creator, obliges everyone to resist the first approaches of tyranny."

If self-defense is an immediate gift of the Creator as Gerry stated, then no government can lawfully usurp such a right. For any government to attempt to do so would be considered an attack upon the people, it would be an open declaration of war by the offending government upon its' own people. The unlawful act should be resisted by the use of just force by the people themselves.

Those with understanding, listen now to these words: *"Unarmed men can only flee from evil, and evil is not defeated by fleeing!!!"*

For the clueless beginning to wake up from their long slumber, if you desire additional information concerning the serious state of our nation you can google the archives of Pastor Chuck Baldwin, former Federal Marshal Greg Evensen and political writer Davy Kidd. In addition you may access the web site of *"Oath Keepers"*, an organization of police and military that have confirmed their allegiance to the Constitutional Laws of America. They have sworn to disobey any unlawful orders from the communist now occupying the White House. They have taken a stand of resistance to the evil that now sits on the horizon.

In addition it might be prudent to order food items from Mountain House Freeze Dried foods on the internet, enough for a period that will sustain you through the coming crisis. A well known radio talk show host stated this week that, *"Actions by the Obama administration are going to ensure hostilities soon in America."* When the conflict begins you won't be going to the grocery store folks.

Since this report was issued a few days ago there have been inquires for additional information concerning monetary policy and what the financial outlook is for the dollar and America. To fully understand the future of the dollar one simply has to research the true definition of monetary inflation. Although this writer has addressed this issue many times, we'll go through it one more time.

With a little knowledge and planning you can still avoid the fate awaiting the unfortunate majority in America and learn why all of the popular financial investments of today are guaranteed methods of confiscation. 401K plans are going to vanish right before your eyes; IRA's will quickly evaporate with no prior warning. Cash assets sitting in checking accounts, savings accounts, mutual funds, government bonds, etc., will all equally leave the unsuspecting masses broke with little hope of financial recovery in their lifetimes.

Pearl Buck, a famous American writer, was in Germany in 1923. She wrote later, *"The cities were still there, the houses not yet bombed and in ruins, but the victims were millions of people. They had lost their fortunes, their savings; they were dazed and inflation-shocked and did not understand how it had happened to them and who the foe was who had defeated them."*

The process is not new, let's go back into our own early history to see that what is about to happen now already happened before in the late 1700"s.

Thomas Jefferson once commented that, "Government monetary treachery relies on peoples' irrational willingness to accept and circulate worthless money substitutes while being under the illusion that they are accepting and saving real money."

John Maynard Keynes replied once, *"By a continuing process of inflation, governments can confiscate, secretly and unobserved, an important part of the wealth of their citizens. There is no subtler, no surer means of overturning the existing basis of society than to debauch the currency. The process engages all the hidden forces of economic law on the side of destruction, and does it in a manner which not one man in a million is able to diagnose!"*

Congressman Ron Paul recently stated, *"It is no exaggeration to say that the survival of Western civilization in general, and America in particular, is at stake in the struggle over standards of value."*

So what does this mean, what are these people talking about? They are talking about the process of inflation that is correctly defined as simply an increase in the money supply, usually created by a central bank or government authority. Inflation is not the price of goods going up; it is the value of the money going down due to government printing presses. The more paper notes they print the more worthless they become. Every newly created note decreases the value of every existing note already in your pocket.

During the Revolutionary War the new colonial government cranked up their printing presses and in a very short period of time increased their money supply from $12 million to $425 million which totally destroyed the value of their currency. The nation was in shambles due to this inflation of the money supply and when the Constitutional Convention was called in 1787 it was for the purpose of setting a gold standard to rebuild the financial structure of the nation. During the convention many delegates addressed the evils of paper money.

Roger Sherman, the author of all the monetary clauses in the constitution stated, *"If what is used as a Medium of Exchange is fluctuating in its Value, it is no better than unjust Weights and Measures, both which are condemned by the Laws of God and Man, and therefore the longest and most universal Custom could never make the use of such a Medium either lawful or reasonable."*

Thomas Paine strongly opposed counterfeiting by the state and said, *"The punishment of a member of Congress who should move for such a law ought to be death!"*

James Wilson, delegate from Pennsylvania advised, *"It will have the most salutary influence on the credit of the United States to remove the possibility of paper money."*

Oliver Ellsworth, the third Chief Justice of the Supreme Court stated, *"This is a favorable moment to shut and bar the door against paper money. The mischiefs of the various experiments which have been made are now fresh in the public mind and have excited the disgust of all the respectable parts of America."*

In 1789, in looking back at the destruction brought on the nation by paper money, statesman Peletiah Webster commented, *"Paper money polluted the equity of our laws, turned them into engines of oppression, corrupted the justice of our public administration, destroyed the fortunes of thousands who had confidence in it, destroyed the trade, husbandry, and manufactures of our country, and went far to destroy the morality of our people!"*

A quote from Congressman Daniel Webster in 1932, "Of *all the contrivances for cheating the laboring classes of mankind, none have been more effectual than that which deludes them with paper money. To maintain a free and strong America we must condemn the use of fraudulent currencies and the robberies committed by depreciated paper!"*

President Andrew Jackson validated this fact in an annual message to Congress in 1836. *"It was the purpose of the Convention to establish a currency consisting of the precious metals. These were adopted by a permanent rule to exclude the use of a perishable medium of exchange such as paper currency."*

Jackson also stated that, *"If the people only understood the rank injustice of our money and banking system, there would be a revolution before morning!"*

OK folks, to make a long story short, when we went off of the gold standard in 1933 we no longer had any disciplinary agent to restrict the printing of paper currency. When on a gold standard, if you do not have the gold to back up the paper being printed, then it does not get printed. Once the gold standard was removed the government has spent, printed more paper, spent and printed more paper until they have reached a point of no return.

Corporations and foreign governments that invest in the U.S. dollar know what the process of inflation is. As the government continues to print, print and print more money these people say, *"Hey, wait a minute, the more paper you print, the more worthless it becomes. We are going to have to receive more of your money now for our products due to the devaluation of your currency by your ever increasing new money creation."* It will finally get to the point where these people will say, *"You have created so much paper currency that it is worthless, we will no longer accept it for our goods and services!"* At that point the dollar will be dumped and abandoned by international money powers and every dollar you own will be worthless overnight. Anything valued in the defunct currency, like 401K's, IRA's, etc., will good up in a puff of smoke.

Backing up now to the Carter days, the Federal Reserve under the direction of President Jimmy Carter was printing money at a staggering pace. The value of our money was declining so fast that retailers were demanding higher prices to compensate for the loss of purchasing power in the inflated currency. When President Ronald Reagan took office he immediately shut down the excessive money creation and delayed the day of reckoning by borrowing money from foreign governments. This was accomplished by the sale of U.S. government bonds and securities. Foreign governments would buy these bonds and securities with the understanding that we would redeem them at some future date with interest. So, a temporary solution was created, if we could borrow money then we would not have to print new money and start fanning the flames of inflation again.

Through this process of borrowing from foreign governments our own government eliminated the need to create new money out of thin air by the use of the printing press. But now we have a new problem materializing on the horizon because all of the world's foreign governments can now see that we are in such heavy debt that we will never be able to redeem any significant amount of the bonds that they hold. Our ability to borrow money is now rapidly coming to an end, our only option remaining is to once again fire up the printing presses, which Obama has done with record speed.

China, the main investor in American dollars is now beginning to dump their dollar holdings and is refusing to invest in any more U.S. bonds or securities. China's Main Sovereign Wealth Fund is currently dumping their dollars in exchange for gold. The gold reserves in China have recently doubled from 454 to 1,054 metric tons of gold. They have invested over $50 Billion in Special Drawing Rights from the

International Monetary Fund which is a reserve currency that has been designated to replace the dollar sometime in the near future. China has also doubled their usual amount of investment in various other commodities as well. All signs that the death of the U.S. dollar is near at hand.

OK let's review, inflation, properly defined, is an increase in the money supply that will ultimately destroy the value of the currency being manipulated leaving the people broke, confused and in a state of anarchy.

Anarchy is always the path to a police state because once the riots begin in the street there is a huge demand by the people themselves to have a military force restore order.

Dr. Henry Kissinger, a progressive (communist) activist, stated at a Bilderberger Conference one time that, *"Today, America would be outraged if UN troops entered Los Angeles to restore order referring to LA riots). Tomorrow they will be grateful! This is especially true if they were told that there were an outside threat from beyond, whether real or promulgated, that threatened their very existence. It is then that all people of the world will plead to deliver them from this evil. The one thing every man fears is the unknown. When presented with this scenario, individual rights will be willingly relinquished for the guarantee of their well being granted to them by the World Government!"*

OK, now that we have a good understanding of what monetary inflation is and what the result is going to be, what we can do to protect our savings and also ourselves in times of crisis. First, consider what real money is. The current generation of Americans does not know what real money is, they have never seen it. Biblical money and the lawful money of this United Stated of America consist of gold and silver coin. After the constitutional convention, gold and silver coin was the law of the land because there has always been just enough gold and silver mined so that it is useful as coinage. Gold and silver were disciplinary agents because if you did not have gold to back up the paper money that was being printed then you did not create the new currency. Gold and silver coin totally eliminates the possibility of inflation because you cannot just create it out of thin air the way printing presses produce paper currency.

Those desiring to invest in gold coins have a couple of options. #1 you can invest in bullion coins which are coins that have never been a currency coin issued by the authority of some government for payment of debt, they are typically one-ounce coins that have a pretty picture stamped upon the face of the coin. Canadian Maple Leaf coins and Chinese Panda coins are two of the most popular coins of this type. #2 you have numismatic coins which were at one time an actual coin issued as money such as a twenty-dollar gold piece. American Double Eagle coins and St. Gauden's coins are of this type of coin. In good condition the premium on these coins can be rather high and more difficult to sell but when gold was confiscated in 1933 the government took the bullion coins and left the numismatic coins alone.

Silver is actually a better value at this point because it is way undervalued compared to gold coins. The two basic types of silver coins to invest in are 1oz. silver rounds and what is referred to as junk silver. 1oz. silver rounds are simply one ounce silver coins with a pretty picture stamped on them, they are .999 pure silver, junk silver is halves, quarters and dimes that were minted prior to 1963 that had 90% silver content in them. If you went into a coin shop to buy a full bag of junk silver that means a bag containing $1,000 face value in coins but it would cost you around $14,000 to purchase because market value is much higher than the face value. You can buy any amount you want, ½ bag or ¼ bag or just a hand full of coins if that is what you want.

Be advised, gold and silver coins are good before a crisis and after a crisis but not during a crisis. In an actual crisis you are going to need food, water, warm clothes, medical supplies and a roof over your head in a preferably rural area. You cannot eat gold and silver coins and during a crisis food will be in short supply. The supplies mentioned here should be your priority before ever investing in coins.

One final bit of information that is going to be useful is to understand that in all issues of law in these United States that the fifty sovereign states have the final word concerning the law. In this country the individual states are sovereign not the federal government. We the people gave birth to the constitution which established the federal government. The federal government is subordinate to the states, not the other way around. A misunderstanding held by many people is that the Supreme Court was established to interpret the constitution, that is not the case. We the people wrote the constitution, we know what it means. We don't need the federal courts telling us what a document means that we wrote ourselves. The function of the Supreme Court is to examine the laws that Congress produces to see if their decrees agree with the constitution. In 1803 the Supreme Court ruled in a case that gives a good example of their true function, the court stated that, *"An act of Congress repugnant to the constitution is not law. When the constitution and an act of Congress are in conflict, the constitution must govern the case to which they both apply. Congress cannot confer on this court any original jurisdiction, The powers of the legislature is defined and limited, and that those limits may not be mistaken or forgotten is the reason the constitution was written!"*

Another example that demonstrates that the sovereignty of this nation lies within the people themselves is the Jury's Prerogative to Nullify Law which means that the jury has a right to judge both the law as well as the fact in controversy. The government decree of law being applied to a case is on trial just as much as the cause which is to be decided.

The prerogative of nullification is not only legitimate, but a praiseworthy right of the jury as well. Prerogative nullification is a mechanism that permits the jury as spokesman for the community's conscience to disregard the strict requirements of man-made law, as well as the judge's instructions to the jury where it finds that those requirements cannot justly be applied in a particular case. Today in the courts this unassailable doctrine is concealed from the jury and is effectively condemned by the judge in the presence of the jury.

Every jury in the land is tampered with and falsely instructed by the judge when it is told it must accept as the law that which is given to them by the court, and that the jury can only decide the facts of the case. This is to destroy the purpose of a common law jury, and to permit the imposition of tyranny upon a people, who otherwise would resist by their juries' refusal to uphold unconstitutional law.

Jurors, who are the only lawful judges in any case being tried by them, are under no obligation to accept or even to be guided by the law as given to them by the government through its agent the "judge"; and there is no rule of common justice or common right by which the twelve juror-judges can be held to consider only the evidence that has met with the government's approval, or by which they can be prevented from taking other facts or circumstances into consideration. They should do, or refuse to do, whatever in their opinion is the best, from the standpoint of preventing or averting injustice. The jurors representing the people are in a legal position to effectively shelter the people from official abuse.

That is why it is necessary that jurors throughout this State and throughout the United States as well, disregard the law as laid down to them by the trial judge, whenever the law is volatile of any of the defendant's inalienable, God-given, common law or Constitutional rights.

If you are ever involved in a jury trial and you feel the statute involved in any criminal case being tried by you is unfair, or that it infringes upon the defendant's natural God-given inalienable or constitutional rights, you must affirm that the offending statute is really no law at all and that the violation of it is no crime at all – for no man is bound to obey an unjust command. Which means if the defendant has disobeyed some man-made criminal statute and the statute itself is unjust, that defendant has committed no crime?

In a jury trial, the twelve jurors are the judges, the court judge is in reality no judge at all, and he is merely in charge of procedure.

The pages of history shine on instances of the jury's exercise of its prerogative to disregard instructions of the judge!!!

Latest Intelligence Reports

The communist's in Washington DC are coordinating their efforts with other communist allies that plan to force Americans into submission. Chinese military front companies have taken control of port facilities on both ends of the Panama Canal and they have developed fourteen shipping ports that completely surround the United States. They have five ports on our west coast, six ports on the east coast and three ports in the Gulf of Mexico. China has also completed the largest container port on earth in Freeport, Bahamas.

Americans should realize that the penetration of U.S. port facilities by Chinese entities is ultimately grounded in military planning and not commercial interests. The Chinese gain of footholds in the Western Hemisphere is obviously related to a clearly developed plan in which Chinese troops have a responsibility for occupying strategic U.S. ground. U.S. border patrols have been reporting to Sheriff Departments around the nation that they have been encountering Chinese regulars making incursions over our southern border for the past several months. Military leaders that remain loyal to these United States of America have recently established the fact that China is preparing to wage a full scale war on America's own home soil sometime in the near future when directed to do so by the traitors that now occupy our government.

Three weeks ago Russian helicopter gunships were seen flying into southern Texas airspace coming out of Mexico. This has been verified by a sheriff's department in the county in which it was observed. Leaders in Texas, Arizona and New Mexico just last week appealed to the Federal Government for troops to be deployed to their southern borders because violence is getting out of control coming up from Mexico. They requested troops that are fully prepared for combat with rules of engagement to include the use of deadly force. This request will no doubt go unanswered.

This week Lt. Colonel John Cotter, the antiterrorism officer for the 144th Fighter Wings Group, stated that Muslims have been purchasing large quantities of pre- paid cell phones at stores around the country. An FBI investigation has determined that these cell phones will be used to detonate bombs that have been pre-positioned throughout the country. FBI has also stated their concerns that a large number of Muslims among us will soon commence the random killing of as many Americans as possible when triggered to do so. Their leader is currently residing in the White House. Last week Obama appointed two radical Muslims to high ranking positions in Homeland Security. He is structuring his thugs and allies to soon wage war against American citizens.

Every human interaction falls into one of two categories, **reason** or **force**. When we own and carry weapons, we cannot be dealt with by force. Those who would have us as slaves must use reason and try to persuade us to accept their communist agenda. However, if they can get us to surrender our weapons, then they no longer need to persuade us. They can use force and we would be powerless to resist. America, do not make the same mistake that all other nations have made in the past that resulted in their total loss of freedom and being the victims of mass murder, THEY WAITED TOO LONG TO RESPOND TO TYRANNY WITH THE USE OF FORCE!!! Thomas Jefferson once commented that, *"The tree of Liberty must on occasion be watered with the blood of Patriots and tyrants; it is its natural manure!"*

Soon the communist's forces in America will be coming for our weapons, if we resist they will bring their allies from all over the globe that they have been positioning for this very task while we were watching football and drinking beer. The majority of Americans have been too busy with life's pleasures and their precious personal desires to notice that the beast is at the gate and it's time to pay the piper. As previously stated in this article, those of you that have been the watchmen upon the wall, those of you who realize that the beast cometh, prepare to defend yourselves, your loved ones and your country. May all the power and force of Heaven be with you and multiply your skills and abilities to wage war against the forces of evil!

Amen.

Patrick Henry before an assembly of fellow countrymen

March 1775

"No man thinks more highly than I do of patriotism... But different men often see the same subject in different lights; and, therefore, I hope it will not be thought disrespectful... if... I should speak forth my sentiments freely, and without reserve. This is no time for ceremony. The question is one of awful moment to this country. Should I keep back my opinions at such time through fear of giving offense, I should consider myself guilty of treason towards my country, and of an act of disloyalty towards my country, and of an act of disloyalty towards the majesty of heaven, which I revere above all things."

It is natural to man to indulge in the illusions of hope. We are apt to shut our eyes against a painful truth, and listen to the song of that siren, till she transforms us into beasts. Is this the part of wise men engaged in a great and arduous struggle for liberty? Are we disposed to be of the number of those who having eyes, see not, and having ears, hear not, the things which so nearly concern their temporal salvation? For my part, whatever anguish of spirit it may cost, I am willing to know the whole truth; to know the worst, and to provide for it."

I have but one lamp by which my feet are guided, and that is the lamp of experience. I know of no way of judging the future but by the past. And judging by the past, I wish to know what there has been to justify the hopes with which gentlemen have been pleased to solace themselves? Is it that insidious smile with which our petition has been lately received? Trust it not, sir; it will prove a snare to your feet. Suffer not yourselves to be betrayed with a kiss. Ask yourselves how this gracious reception comports with those warlike preparations which cover our waters and darken our land... Let us not deceive ourselves... These are the implements of war and subjugation

— the last arguments to which king resort. I ask what means this martial array if its purpose be not to force us to submission? Can gentlemen assign any other possible motive for it? And what have we to oppose them? Shall we try argument? Sir, we have been trying that for ten years last. Have we anything new to offer upon the subject? Nothing. We have held the subject up in every light of which was capable; but it has been all in vain. Shall we resort to entreaty and humble supplication? Let us not deceive ourselves longer. Sir, we have done everything that could be done to divert the storm which is now coming on."

"We have petitioned; we have remonstrated; we have supplicated; we have prostrated ourselves before the throne, and have implored its interposition. Our petitions have been slighted; our remonstrances have produced additional violence and insult; our supplications have been disregarded; and we have been spurned, with contempt, from the foot of the throne. In vain, after these things, we may indulge the fond hope of peace and reconciliation. There is no longer any room for hope. If we wish to be free; if we mean to preserve inviolate those inestimable privileges for which we have been so long contending; if we mean not basely to abandon the noble struggle in which we have been so long engaged, and which we have pledged ourselves never to abandon until the glorious object of our contest shall be obtained; we must fight! I repeat, sir, we must fight! An appeal to arms and the God of Hosts is all that has left us!"

"They tell us that we are weak, unable to cope with so formidable an adversary. But when shall we be stronger? Will it be next week or next year? Will it be when we are totally disarmed, and when a guard shall be stationed in every house? Shall we gather strength by irresolution and inaction? Shall we acquire the means of effectual resistance by lying supinely on our backs and hugging the delusive phantom of hope until our enemies shall have bound us hand and foot?"

"Sir, we are not weak if we make proper use of those means the God of Nature hath placed in our power... Millions of people armed in the holy cause of liberty, and in such a country as that which we possess, are invincible by any force which our enemy can send against us. Besides, sir,

we shall not fight our battles alone. There is a just God who presides over the destinies of nations, and who will raise up friends to fight our battles for us. The battle, sir, is not to the strong alone; it is to the vigilant, the active, and the brave. Besides, sir, we have no election. If we were base enough to desire it, it is now too late to retire from the contest. There is no retreat, but in submission and slavery! Our chains are forged. Their clanking may be heard on the plains of Boston! The war is inevitable – and let it come! I repeat, sir, let it come!"

"It is in vain to extenuate the matter further. Gentlemen may cry peace, peace, but there is no peace. The war is actually begun! The next gale that sweeps from the north will bring to our ears the clash of resounding arms! Our brethren are already in the field! Why stand we here idle? What is it gentlemen wish? What would they have? Is life so dear, or peace so sweet, as to be purchased at the price of chains and slavery? Forbid it, Almighty God! I know not what course others may take; but as for me, give me LIBERTY or give me DEATH!"

In closing I'd like to mention recent comments made by Former Federal Marshal Greg Evensen. A few weeks ago Mr. Evensen stated that, "Your republic is gone; you are now living in a socialist/ communist state. The noose is rapidly encircling the neck of America! You have no concept about how bad this is going to get!"

The former Federal Marshal continued, "Total information awareness is in place. The communists in our government have already calculated the areas of most resistance, the most disruptive elements of the American population that will resist tyranny through force of arms. The communists have targeted these individuals for rapid extermination."

"Be advised, a large per cent of our own police and military are poised to invade the American people. Over the past ten years, American civilian law enforcement has been militarized in preparation for engaging the elements of anticipated civilian resistance. Over the course of history, how many millions have been slaughtered by their own countrymen who were just following orders?"

"In the past few weeks, military leaders have been gathered by the Obama administration to report on their operational status and readiness to deal with anticipated hostility from American citizens. The seal on their standing orders was broken and these leaders were informed that action is imminent. Obama recently signed an executive order allowing "Interpol", an international police organization, to start occupying positions on American soil. The occupation of America by communist foreign troops has already begun."

"Confidential discussions with FBI resources indicate that the FBI has hardened many of their main facilities across the nation in preparation for a major national crisis. It is the full belief of our FBI that civil war is just over the horizon and that China will attack our mainland in the midst of this crisis. These hardened facilities have been designated to be the final fall back positions for the defense of America against the invasion forces of Beijing!"

Tim Lamb comments May 8, 2010 *"Keep in mind, my fellow Americans, that modern history is the science of human misfortune in which few people have been spared from mass violence."*

"Our current Obama administration is full of individuals with an unrepeated criminal past just waiting for the opportunity to unleash hell on earth once again. To fertilize the killing fields with the blood of innocent people once more!"
Facts Concerning Tim

"Mr. Lamb is one of the nation's leading authorities on national and international monetary policy. During the past twenty years he has educated people nationwide through conferences, national radio broadcasts and internet publications. He is an accomplished research specialist in areas concerning history, geo-political issues and constitutional law. In addition he has several years of medical study in the areas of natural health and healing." Lt. Col. R. J.

"Fifteen years ago Mr. Lamb warned us of things to come in our lifetimes and we did not believe it possible, now it is here and upon us. Now when

Tim says something we listen! His insight and knowledge concerning national and international events is a powerful tool to be utilized in preparing for the near future." Brig. Gen. L. H.

Mr. Lamb was country raised in southeast Kansas. He married his post high school sweetheart and now has two daughters plus a grandson and granddaughter. He is a small animal lover and owns a Blue Lynx Rag Doll female cat named Sasha. She is his loyal companion and lap kitty. His hobbies include many years of training in martial arts, knife fighting and close quarters combat handgun tactics. He has trained with one of the nation's leading police and military professionals in armed and unarmed conflict resolution.

Also Mr. Lamb has spent a significant amount of time engaged in field command and control operations with former Special Forces Green Beret and Army Ranger personnel. He has conducted firearms training in several states including Oklahoma, Kansas, Texas, Arkansas and New York.

Mr. Lamb also spends a fair amount of time in the area of long-range rifle rules of engagement and conduct in hostile environments. He is an experienced weapons specialist holding extensive knowledge of German HK91, Belgian FN-FAL and FNAR rifles. Also with Springfield Armory M1 Garand, Colt CAR 15 and AR 15 rifles, as well as Russian AK47, SKS and Beretta Cx4 Storm carbines.

Handgun experience includes Colt .45, Kimber Tactical .45 and Heckler & Koch USP Tactical .45. Knife choices include the SOG tech Bowie, the Zero Tolerance 0200 Military Tactical folding knife and the World War II era K-Bar Blades.

Night vision equipment is cost prohibitive to a lot of individuals but to those that can afford it the ATN PS-22 night vision optical system is a must because the bad boys all engage at night folks. The ATN PS-22 night vision optics with 3rd generation image intensifier clamps right on to the front of your daytime scope for night operations. This setup allows the shooter to go from day to night operations in less than 30 seconds without tools. Eye relief and zero remain unchanged around the clock. Bad boys don't fear the night but they do fear the one that hunts at night. If you can afford it, get it!!!

This writer's favorite black rifle and weapon of choice is the Fabrique National Automatic Rifle (FNAR). The weapon is a Belgian designed .308 caliber rifle with a fluted, hard chrome lined barrel, making it light and well balanced. Mr. Lamb's personal weapon is equipped with a Burris Xtreme Tactical Scope utilizing an Illuminated Ballistic Mil-Dot Reticle which allows for all of your day and low light shooting endeavors. A Harris Bi-Pod produces a very stable platform for when you really need to reach out there for the long shots.

Chapter 23

Historical Documentation of Christian Conduct

During Times of Tyranny!

By Timothy Lamb Sept. 6, 2010

Turning Points

Tyranny always wears a velvet glove over its iron fist until all preparations have been laid and the steel trap is snapped down upon the necks of the unsuspecting masses. **The Rev. Samuel Langdon** confirms the fact of how quickly you can move from thinking all is well to realizing the party's over. In 1775 he stated, *"Our late happy government is changed into the terrors of military execution. Our firm opposition to the establishment of an arbitrary system is called rebellion, and we are to expect no mercy but to yield property and life at discretion. This we are resolved at all events not to do, and therefore we have taken up arms in our own defense, and all the colonies are united in the great cause of liberty."*

Both their faith and their reason led the ministers to believe in government by **Compact or Constitution**. Even God rules in accordance with the constitution of natural laws. Even God made His compact with Noah, Moses and Joshua. If God, who rules by just laws anyway, made His compact with man, how natural and essential it is for imperfect human rulers to rule according to a written constitution setting forth their duties and limiting their power. **Thomas Barnard** stated in 1763, "All power has its foundation in compact and mutual consent or else it proceeds from fraud or violence."

Rev. John Tucker commented in 1771, *"Submission is due to all constitutional laws, whether they suit the present interest of individuals or not. Unlimited submission, however, is not due to government in a free state. There are certain boundaries beyond which submission cannot be justly required, nor is therefore due. These limits are marked out, and fixed, by the known, established, and fundamental laws of the state. These laws being consented to by the governing power, confine as well as direct its operation and influence, and are the connecting band between authority and obedience."*

Those of you who have personal beliefs that your Christianity requires passive submission with no resistance to evil, then understand that your belief system is the same type that the German and Russian Christians had that gave birth to Hitler and Stalin. All it takes for evil to prevail is for good people to do nothing. To remain silent in the face of radical corruption makes cowards of men and leads to the mass murder of millions.

Realize this people, as previously mentioned; Obama has never been a legitimate authority in these United States of America. All of Congress knows that this fraud is ineligible to sit in the office of president due to the fact that he is not a natural born citizen. He is a radical, Marxist Communist with an agenda to destroy the United States. There is a big difference between lawful authority and a criminal usurper like Obama. The problem is that many of us are too ignorant to know the difference!!!

Continuing with Biblical examples of resistance to tyranny consider Abraham, whose own sense of justice initiated the use of force. There was no divine command given or needed for Abraham to know that as his "brother's keeper," he had to deliver Lot. After he returned, God put His stamp of approval on Abraham's actions by having Melchizidek, the high priest, bless him. The New Testament's approval of Melchizidek's blessing of Abraham prevents anyone from saying that Melchizidek's blessing was not a divine blessing.

It is assumed by some that only wars or defensive actions fought in self- defense are just, that it would be immoral to attack another unless attacked first. The problem with the above theory is that Abraham's use of force was not in self- defense. Chedorlaomer was not attacking him. Abraham was initiating the conflict by pursuing and attacking a tyrannical enemy. In this light, it is clear that wars or armed responses to tyranny can sometimes be viewed as perfectly just and righteous.

On many occasions throughout the Bible, God's people used armed force to overthrow tyranny. Scriptures clearly show that God never viewed a tyrannical power as a legitimate government. Just because an elite group was in power because of their weapons, they were not viewed as the government ordained of God, because God never ordains tyranny. Thus, God never commands His people to view tyranny as valid authority.

When a government abandons its delegated sphere of responsibility, overstepping its bounds and invading the sphere of the church or the family, it is no longer a divinely appointed government, it has become a tyrannical power. A government is viewed as being tyrannical when it consistently punishes the righteous and protects and rewards the wicked, when it consistently invades other spheres and seeks to dominate all life by sheer force. Such a government is not ordained of God and should be resisted by the believer.

It is the duty of Christians to resist tyranny because tyranny seeks to take Christ's place as the Lord of all of life. This resistance can be either passive or active, depending on the situation. When oppressed people desire to depose a tyrant and political recourse is closed to them, then force may be used. Our early American forefathers believed that if we take the many scriptural examples of such action seriously, all wars or revolutions fought to gain freedom from tyranny are just.

The churches in colonial America were the driving force behind the American Revolution because of their Puritan theology of resistance to tyranny. They felt that they had a divine mandate to resist tyranny with their lives if necessary. The liberty we have enjoyed in the Free World until now is due to their sacrifice.

Historically, the most authentic servants of Christ have always been the worst enemies of tyranny and the oppressor.

THOSE OF YOU WHO HAVE THE IDEA THAT RESISTANCE TO EVIL IS OUTSIDE THE REALM OF CHRISTIAN CONDUCT, PLEASE DO NOT CELEBRATE THE 4TH OF JULY EVER AGAIN BECAUSE YOU ARE CELEBRATING THE MEMORY OF MEN WHO USED ARMED FORCE TO RESIST TYRANNY!!!

As the tyrannical nature of our current den of vipers continues to attack this nation of free people, decide now who you will chose to serve, your time is short!!!

Revision 2: 8/4/2011

A country where the citizens are armed and trained in the use of those arms is a country where the government cannot maintain a monopoly of power. The armed citizen preserves freedom by ensuring the duty to defend one's country would not be delegated to a select and potentially dangerous few such as our own government which now wishes to force us into a world government run by elitists who care nothing about human rights!

Our Constitutional Republic was designed to prevent tyranny by the Sovereign power remaining in the hands of the people. The Constitution is the highest law in the land, not the decrees initiated by the criminals now occupying Washington DC. Our own United States Supreme Court testified to this fact when it ruled in 1809 that, *"An act of Congress repugnant to the constitution is not law. When the constitution and an act of Congress are in conflict, the constitution must govern the case to which they both apply. Congress cannot confer on this court any original jurisdiction. The powers of the legislature are defined and limited, and that those limits may not be mistaken or forgotten is the reason the constitution was written."*

From the Sixteenth American Jurisprudence, Second Edition, Section 256: "The general rule is that an unconstitutional statue, though having the form and name of law, is in reality no law, but is wholly void, and ineffective for any purpose; since unconstitutionality dates from the time of its enactment, and not merely from the date of the decision so branding it. An unconstitutional law, in legal contemplation, is as inoperative as if it had never been passed. Such a statute leaves the question it purports to settle just as it would be had the statute not been enacted."

"Since an unconstitutional law is void, the general principles follow that it imposes no duties, confers no rights, creates no office, bestows no power or authority to anyone, affords no protection, and justifies no acts performed under it."

"A void act cannot be legally consistent with a valid one. An unconstitutional law cannot operate to supersede any existing valid law. Indeed, insofar as a statute runs counter to the fundamental law of the land, it is superseded thereby. No one is bound to obey an unconstitutional law and no courts are bound to enforce it!"

The most scholarly authority in matters of American law was **William Blackstone,** who once stated, *"No man or set of men can create law. Man has no power, no authority, and no jurisdiction to make law. He can and he is supposed to enforce and obey God's law. Civil servants have no delegated authority to legalize crime, make lawful acts illegal, or illegal acts lawful. Man must obey the Law! This means he must obey God! To obey men in violation of God's law would be the highest form or treason against God!"*

"When Congress, state legislatures, or city governments pass ordinances that would confiscate a man's labor, rob his children of their inheritance, or redistribute the wealth to the lazy and wicked, and support abortion and sodomy, Godly men are compelled to refuse to comply with such ordinances. No man can serve two masters; either he will serve God or the State."

"Law is the embodiment of those powers created by God for the protection of life, liberty and property. When government ceases to fulfill the proper role of government, primarily the protection of life, liberty and property or even worse yet, when it becomes the force under the color of law to kill, imprison and steal from its citizens, then men not only may, but have a duty to alter, remove or destroy the persons or the form of government which perpetrates such crimes against the citizenry."

It's a mistake to think you can stop the Marxist freight train that's barreling across our land by reasoning with or trying to persuade the enemy to desist. You cannot!!! The Obama Administration is currently pushing to ratify an international treaty with foreign governments in the U.N. that will totally ban all small arms in the United States over night. This will be accomplished through the new **Super Congress** once they have established their role as the new gods of power and after they have set a standard of law denying any voice or opposition by other members of Congress. Foreign troops are already stationed at U.S. military bases that will be used to enforce the ban and confiscate weapons. Sheriff departments all across the central and southern U.S. have already war gamed out the scenario of civil war that will commence once the attempt to disarm Americans begins.

The criminal administration of Obama, along with the new homeland security leaders, has already publicly stated that any American that believes in the Bible and the U.S. Constitution is considered as enemy combatants to be eradicated. In the latest edition of the U.S. Army/ Marine Corps Counterinsurgency Field Manual, Chapter 1, page 2, it states that the government needs to eliminate those extremists whose beliefs prevent them from ever reconciling with the government. That means they intend to slaughter those they consider enemy combatants when they feel they can do so effectively! Give it your best shot boys!

If we allow ourselves to be disarmed in this country we will have unleashed a spirit of murder that will follow that the world has never seen before. In the near future there will be no compromise, no quarter given, and no peaceful co- existence. It will be death to one culture or the other, communism or Free America! Soon will be a time to take no prisoners, the order of the day will soon come to shoot on sight the enemies of liberty. So, prepare to lock and load sons of the Republic. Once again you will be called upon to sacrifice in order for the righteousness of Haven to be maintained on the earth.

Chapter 24

The Melting Pot Has Melted

Turning Points

"If you care if a thief breaks into your home and steals your possessions, then you should really care if a thief breaks into your country and steals your freedoms!" Jan t…

A country of many peoples, from many counties, created for all peoples, religions and colors, all seeking the freedoms and Liberty of one nation full of opportunity, hope and safety to join that which they did not have. They have crossed the line and the meaning of the Melting Pot and have created discourse for all Americans.

The English language taught across this globe and in most, if not all countries, a must learn language if one was to succeed. It has been subjected to outside immigrants that care not. They have no desire to blend into the Melting Pot but have chosen to melt into the pot and transform it into what is important for them and only them.

The Melting Pot has melted. It is no longer a place for all people for there is no one place that those that seek to become part of the pot can gain a foot hold in the overall freedom of which most in the world so seek. The transformation of a Nation has been desecrated by those that seek not Liberty but seek their kind in transforming that which they want to enjoy…

Traditions are important for all people that have crossed the waters or have crossed the borders, some legal and most illegal, but to still dwell in that which they fled makes one wonder what their true motives were. There were many looking for Freedom and Liberty but would not or cared not to learn the culture, language, and history of this new land (the United States) they enjoy.

They are transforming the culture, history, and language into that which they fled, instead of blending into a country of much history, tradition and language. They continue to seek in their daily lives that which they despised. It is most disturbing. Why would a people leave a country that creates poverty, dismay, and murders of its citizens, police officers and other innocent citizens not want to blend into a country they want to dwell?

So, what is the purpose? I find this form of invasion misguided from where it comes. The United States will not survive unless this style of attitudes among the invaders is squashed.

Due to years of political correctness the invaders have slowly transformed this country's founding and principles into a country of: "We feel sorry for you, so bring yourself across that border. Bring your language, habits and history and at all cost, please remove that which the United Sates has had in place for centuries,

and please replace it with what you want for yourself, your friends and your family. "

The United States really did not need it because your feelings are far more important than a few documents that were written to protect all legal citizens of the United States.

One other thing I forgot: "Please abuse our medical systems for your gain and at all costs get a driver license under false identify, and by all means, do not get insurance for the legal driving citizens will pay and absorb the cost on your behalf. "

One more thing: "Please have your baby born in our country so he/she may become a citizen of the United States entitled to all this country has to offer for a legal citizen and by all means because of that birth on the soil of a free people, bring across all the family members that are associated with that family."

After all, we just want you to feel welcome in a country you should have been arrested for violating our laws. However, we forgive you, your baby, your husband and most important your family.

The American people once stood for the documents and the founder's intent for a Nation to survive that which would prove to come in short order. Today, that day has come. The so-called PC police aka Political Correctness, has circumvented all that was created. There lies not a melting pot, but a pot melted.

The question for today:

"Will the United Sates citizens manage to hold on to that which was given, or will they continue down the path so directed and mandated by those that have not comment or control but desire that which they want from those of ill begotten measures for self-gain and fulfillment?"

Chapter 25

Do You Know Your Bill of Rights

Turning Points

The Bill of Rights contains the first 10 amendments to the Constitution. Written by James Madison because several states were seeking greater constitutional protection for individual liberties, the Bill of Rights lists specific prohibitions on governmental powers. Madison was strongly influenced by Mason who wrote the Virginia Declaration of Rights.

This was one of many points of contention between Federalists and Anti- Federalists was the Constitution's lack of a bill of rights that would place specific limits on government power. Federalist would argue that the Constitution did not need a bill of rights, because the people and the states kept any powers not given to the federal government to the people. However, Anti-Federalists held that a bill of rights was necessary to safeguard individual liberties…

On that point one might suggest that if not for the bill of rights, governing powers may have trampled on the rights of the people when government achieved power over the states and the people. This is where we are today, a governing body that has circumvented the Constitution and are attempting to remove the rights of the people, including the bill of rights.

Currently our Liberty and our Republic are in shambles, reading the bill of rights might bring some semblance to the war at hand. The war between an overpowering Federal Government against the States and the People. It is self evident what is happening in Arizona with border issue and a suit filed by the Federal Government against a State of these United States to resend and back off of the states' rights to protect the citizens of the state of Arizona against illegal immigration.

The Bill of Rights

Amendment I

Congress shall make no law respecting an establishment of religion, or prohibiting the free exercise thereof; or abridging the freedom of speech, or of the press; or the right of the people peaceably to assemble, and to petition the government for a redress of grievances.

Amendment II

A well regulated militia, being necessary to the security of a free state, the right of the people to keep and bear arms, shall not be infringed.

Amendment III

No soldier shall, in time of peace be quartered in any house, without the consent of the owner, nor in time of war, but in a manner to be prescribed by law.

Amendment IV

The right of the people to be secure in their persons, houses, papers, and effects, against unreasonable searches and seizures, shall not be violated, and no warrants shall issue, but upon probable cause, supported by oath or affirmation, and particularly describing the place to be searched, and the persons or things to be seized.

Amendment V

No person shall be held to answer for a capital, or otherwise infamous crime, unless on a presentment or indictment of a grand jury, except in cases arising in the land or naval forces, or in the militia, when in actual service in time of war or public danger; nor shall any person be subject for the same offense to be twice put in jeopardy of life or limb; nor shall be compelled in any criminal case to be a witness against himself, nor be deprived of life, liberty, or property, without due process of law; nor shall private property be taken for public use, without just compensation.

Amendment VI

In all criminal prosecutions, the accused shall enjoy the right to a speedy and public trial, by an impartial jury of the state and district wherein the crime shall have been committed, which district shall have been previously ascertained by law, and to be informed of the nature and cause of the accusation; to be confronted with the witnesses against him; to have compulsory process for obtaining witnesses in his favor, and to have the assistance of counsel for his defense.

Amendment VII

In suits at common law, where the value in controversy shall exceed twenty dollars, the right of trial by jury shall be preserved, and no fact tried by a jury, shall be otherwise reexamined in any court of the United States, than according to the rules of the common law.

Amendment VIII

Excessive bail shall not be required, nor excessive fines imposed, nor cruel and unusual punishments inflicted.

Amendment IX

The enumeration in the Constitution, of certain rights, shall not be construed to deny or disparage others retained by the people.

Amendment X

The powers not delegated to the United States by the Constitution, nor prohibited by it to the states, are reserved to the states respectively, or to the people.

The founders new there would be a time when the people and the government they created would be tested and to that point the time is here.

The Bill of Rights is a list of limits of government power. Currently our government has exceeded that power with the Obama Care mandate and the suits filed against states trying to protect the rights of the state and their citizens from illegal immigration and the Obama Care Mandate.

One example, the natural right to be free from unreasonable government intrusion in one's home was safeguarded by the Fourth Amendment's warrant requirements.

That being said, what is happening at airports and other venues across our land when TSA agents can fondle or use X-ray machines to intrude against a person right to unreasonable searches and seizures. This would be a violation of the fourth amendment. The lists go on and on but the sheeple continue to let it happen.

In the Constitution, are principles and among those principles were included checks and balances, individual rights, liberty, limited government, natural rights, republican government and popular sovereignty.

We are at a turning point in our history. There are two choices at hand, one that is leading us to dark side of government and total control based on political objectives, and one that is seeking followers towards the Republic we once had.

There is still hope for our country and our Republic. One might think that the Freedom fighters of today are dreamers but that is not the case at all. One must believe in what we are and what we can still be if we only stand on the principles that were given by the founders and the documents they created with Gods hand.

Choices?

Chapter 26

Protecting Our Rights

Turning Points

Every day we awake with hope, challenges and opportunity. We put trust in individuals of our government and the actions they take will affect our lives as Americans. We elected them to represent us and safeguard this great land in which we live.

It has long past that the people have questions regarding the efforts of the elected few that compassed this venue. It appears from all sides that most are not in like state. The challenge for the people and the documents created are as dry skin on the carcass of our Liberty and our Republic.

It is with great aspirations that government in its effort seems determined to help a few people while restricting the rights of the WHOLE and placing more government controls on the body POLITIC.

The American people give the congress, president and the justice's great power, and opportunity. With that power, comes great responsibility to protect the rights of the people and not a state or their office.

WE the People must at all cost rein in this intrusion of our Liberty and our Republic and demand they focus on the Rights given to protect the people from the government. Will They?

The People must understand their Rights first, before they can even phantom Protecting them. Most, if not all have no knowledge of the Rights given to them.

It is somewhat inspiring for many Americans to actually question what governments do to people but on the same point the unknown will never be understood by some and only favored by those of knowledge and understanding.

This land we sit upon is a most sacred land, blessed by GOD and ordained by his message. Yet, we continue to question it.

The Rights of the People are in the writing of the documents of our Republic and Liberty. We the people must understand this venue in order to correct its miss giving by those chosen to represent the people!

What we are facing is a battle of the minds. The concepts and motivations that we are fighting for and what we are fighting against.

We can continue to be padlocked from our Liberty and burn in the hell that has been created or we can break the lock and force action from the people and rights given towards those that govern.

We do not need shovel ready jobs as Obama has stated! We need Patriots and a congress that believe in this country to do their job regardless of party, focused on the Rights that protect us all!

We can be on a lone horse carrying the flag of this Nation against tyrants that are consumed to destroy her. Who will be at hand, carrying that FLAG is yet to be determined. But that time is near!

The awaking has come and with it will be the People focused on Liberty, our Rights and OUR REPUBLIC!

Choices?

Chapter 27

The Heart of Champions

Turning Points

Champions for Liberty do not bring forward their message every day. It was just 230 years past that we had Champions in those that stood the ground for our Liberty and our Republic.

There have been many heated debates regarding the founder's motives and what they gave us. We were given a Constitution which was and still is the structure that holds the country together. It has been the glue that has held these states from falling apart through rebellion. Our founders knew this and that is why they called it: a "grand experiment"; and even Franklin commented: "It's a Republic…if you can keep it." At one point in our history there were even assessments that maybe the only solution was a 'benevolent dictator" a life-long "kingship" offered to George Washington, which he refused!

It was just a few years later, some 90 years or less, we had a Civil War to save the union. So, who and what are we as a nation? What are we fighting for in the political venue and why are we having this fight?

There are two sides in the debate. Both are polar opposites in the realm of reason. One is based clearly on our history as a nation and reliance in the future on all those things that have made it great in the past. The other is based on the unproven or disproven fantasy of social theory that holds no guarantees of success because their vision of the future is just as cloudy as their vision of our past and our future.

The voices of the people are being heard all across this land in commentary, Face book, Freedom Torch and tweets, posted in the cloudy vision to the mindless few that are demanding more from the government not knowing what they are asking will be the worst of all worst in the end.

Rural areas of this country have long since prepared for the onslaught of those escaping and seeking venue in the rural communities they so despised. When times become so difficult in the suburbs of America they will be fleeing like maggots on a dead carcass looking for a safe haven in an unknown world of their brethrens (aka the fly over states, communities and towns).

The Heart of Champions is compelled and driven by the history, the documents that created her and with passions, to right the wrongs that have driven her into this cloudy mist we currently stand.

The awaking has come and with it will be the People focused on Liberty, our Rights and OUR REPUBLIC!

Choices?

Chapter 28

WHAT HAPPENED TO COMMON SENSE

Turning Points

Today we mourn the passing of a beloved old friend, **Common Sense,** who has been with us for many years. No one knows for sure how old he was, since his birth records were long ago lost in bureaucratic red tape. He will be remembered as having cultivated such valuable lessons as:

- Knowing when to come in out of the rain;
- Why the early bird gets the worm;
- Life isn't always fair;
- and maybe it was my fault..

Common Sense lived by simple, sound financial policies (don't spend more than you can earn) and reliable strategies (adults, not children, are in charge).

His health began to deteriorate rapidly when well-intentioned but overbearing regulations were set in place. Reports of a 6-year-old boy charged

with sexual harassment for kissing a classmate; teens suspended from school for using mouthwash after lunch; and a teacher fired for reprimanding an unruly student, only worsened his condition.

Common Sense lost ground when parents attacked teachers for doing the job that they themselves had failed to do in disciplining their unruly children.

It declined even further when schools were required to get parental consent to administer sun lotion or a paracetamol to a student; but

could not inform parents when a student became pregnant and wanted to have an abortion.

Common Sense lost the will to live as the churches became businesses; and criminals received better treatment than their victims.

Common Sense took a beating when you couldn't defend yourself from a burglar in your own home and the burglar could sue you for assault.

Common Sense finally gave up the will to live, after a woman failed to realize that a steaming cup of coffee was hot. She spilled a little in her lap, and was promptly awarded a huge settlement.

Common Sense was preceded in death, by his parents, Truth and Trust, by his wife, Discretion, by his daughter, Responsibility, and by his son, Reason.

He is survived by his 4 stepbrothers;
I Know My Rights
I Want It Now
Someone Else Is To Blame
I'm A Victim

Not many attended his funeral because so few realized he was gone. If you still remember him, pass this on. If not, join the majority and do nothing.

"I really do not who wrote this comment regarding Common Sense, but I would love to set down with the person and have a cup of coffee or glass of tea and have a common sense conversation, regarding Common Sense."

Chapter 29

The Eve of Rebellion – 2012

In chapter one of this book some several pages back, I talked about the eve of Rebellion in 1773. What happened then is paramount as to what is happening today. This President (Obama), his czars, and this congress along with all the liberal, progressive media are painting on the landscape of our Republic and our Liberty should be the focus by the people and the saving grace of this Republic.

I do not at this time think the people are totally asleep and without wisdom. Surely they see it. Even with all the controllers levity on the people they must come to terms when looking at the picture as it is being painted.

There is a great awaking in these United States, when a government has created more debt, of 6 trillion, along with a willing Congress, in less than four years, who should be ashamed for what they have done.

To tell you the true in retrospect, the militia of 1773, were not trained as the militias of today, but the meaning is under laid in a democracy not a Republic.

In chapter one of this book on page 14, I wrote "there is much more to this story that would lead up to the Founding of this country, the Declaration and the battles for Independence and Liberty for all Americans, not just a few but ALL!

Is the United States Constitution a sham!

Samuel Johnson, a conservative, famed for his English dictionary, was no friend of Americans,

Chapter 30

Will this be the Final Turning Point?

Turning Points

_"Children of tomorrow, We apologize to you, on behalf of those in my time, for the things we did not do.

We didn't stop the tyrants, so your fate could be prevented,

We watched them steal our freedom, by our silence we consented.

We didn't choose to circumvent, the doom you've not escaped, while the Bill of Rights was murdered, and the Constitution raped!

Some of us were lazy, others too afraid, to think about our children, the ones we have betrayed!"

"I guess we were too busy, to be concerned or care, to try to ease the burden, of the chains we made you wear.

We could have been good Shepherds, when the wolf got in the fold, but watched the flame of freedom die, instead, and left you in the cold.

We changed our great Republic, which was forged in Liberty, to a socialistic welfare state, we called Democracy."

"I'm sorry we were timid, my selfish generation, we left you but a remnant, of a free and prosperous nation.

I'm sorry for our actions, like cowards we behaved, we could have left you freedom, and instead you are enslaved.

Children of tomorrow, descendants of our land, I'm sorry we allowed this, the fate you now withstand."

Chapter 31

The Bill of NO Rights

The Bill of No Rights

"We the sensible people of the United States, in an attempt to help everyone get along, must restore some semblance of justice, avoid more riots, keep our nation safe, promote positive behavior, and secure the blessings of debt-free liberty to ourselves and our great-great-great-grandchildren, hereby try one more time to ordain and establish some common sense guidelines for the terminally whiny, guilt ridden, delusional, and other liberal bed-wetter's.. We hold these truths to be self evident: that a whole lot of people are confused by the Bill of Rights and are so dim they require a Bill of NON-Rights"

ARTICLE I:

You do not have the right to a new car, big screen TV, or any other form of wealth. More power to you if you can legally acquire them, but no one is guaranteeing anything.

ARTICLE II:

You do not have the right to never be offended. This country is based on freedom, and that means freedom for everyone   not just you! You may leave the room, turn the channel, express a different opinion, etc; but the world is full of idiots, and probably always will be.

ARTICLE III:

You do not have the right to be free from harm. If you stick a screwdriver in your eye, learn to be more careful; do not expect the tool manufacturer to make you and all your relatives independently wealthy.

ARTICLE IV:

You do not have the right to free food and housing. Americans are the most charitable people to be found, and will gladly help anyone in need, but we are quickly growing weary of subsidizing generation after generation of professional couch potatoes who achieve nothing more than the creation of another generation of professional couch potatoes.

ARTICLE V:

You do not have the right to free health care. That would be nice, but from the looks of public housing, we're just not interested in public health care.

ARTICLE VI:

You do not have the right to physically harm other people. If you kidnap, rape, intentionally maim, or kill someone, don't be surprised if the rest of us want to see you fry in the electric chair or lethal injection.

ARTICLE VII:

You do not have the right to the possessions of others. If you rob, cheat, or coerce away the goods or services of other citizens, don't be surprised if the rest of us get together and lock you away in a place where you still won't have the right to a big screen color TV or a life of leisure.

ARTICLE VIII:

You do not have the right to a job. All of us sure want you to have a job, and will gladly help you along in hard times, but we expect you to take advantage of the opportunities of education and vocational training laid before you to make yourself useful. (AMEN!)

ARTICLE IX:

You do not have the right to happiness. Being an American means that you have the right to PURSUE happiness, which by the way, is a lot easier if you are unencumbered by an overabundance of idiotic laws created by those of you who were confused by the Bill of Rights.

ARTICLE X:

This is an English speaking country. We don't care where you are from, English is our language. Learn it or go back to wherever you came from! (Lastly)

ARTICLE XI:

You do not have the right to change our country's history or heritage. This country was founded on the belief in one true God. And yet, you are given the freedom to believe in any religion, any faith, or no faith at all; with no fear of persecution. The phrase IN GOD WE TRUST is part of our heritage and history, and if you are uncomfortable with it, TOUGH!

Just think it's about time common sense is allowed to flourish. Sensible people of the United States speak out because if you do not, who will?[4]

"The life that conquers is the life that moves with a steady resolution and persistence toward a predetermined goal. Those who succeed are those who have thoroughly learned the immense importance of plan in life, and the tragic brevity of time."
W.J. Davison

"The walls of our homes have fallen. Once there was a church of hope and it has turned and burned into a destructive force against those that have given all in order to protect those that would march against those who will now be laying in soil of the founders. Pray, for maybe they will see the wisdom of the Father..."
Terry W. Bettis

---

[4] http://www.lrudel.com/bill.htm

"The greatest gift you will ever receive is the gift of loving and believing in yourself. Guard this gift with your life. It is the only thing that will ever truly be yours. "

Tiffany Loren Rowe

"If successful people have one common trait, it's an utter lack of cynicism. The world owes them nothing. They go out and find what they need without asking for permission; they're driven, talented, and work through negatives by focusing on the positives."

– Mike Zimmerman

'The American Spirit, vol: 1, by Bailey

After the Chapters
Regarding today's events

My Personal Thoughts and Comments

If You Are Christian and a Patriot

In the year 2012

Commentary: 01/04/2012

If you are a Christian and a Patriot then you have become the targets of the radical Muslims, illegal aliens, War lords, Gangs from all backgrounds led by the drug wars and their motives and most important a government that has excepted an Oligarchic Dictatorship, for control.

In their attempt to take control, the one thing in the equation left out, was a Christian and a Patriot.

The Liberals, Progressives, Communists, Wall Street marchers, and Radicals running rampant in this land have left behind, for just cause, the Christian and Patriots. That will be their misgiving of their own demise.

I remember a battle in Texas in 1836, it became known as: "Remember the Alamo" when Texans were fighting against an over empowering force from the Mexican army, to create a country. Two Hundred men stood willing to face them, while 183 in the Alamo would pass during the 13 days of battle, but they took with them 600 among the count.

If you are Christian and a Patriot is it time to run through the neighborhoods and look at the drug deals going on? Is it time to visit the borders and see what is happening? The threads of our freedoms are being stretched beyond its ability to sustain. If one could see it, they might understand why there is much to do to fix it.

I for one am a Christian and also a Patriot. I have no fear from radicals, nor do I fear their motives. I will meet them with like force should they choose to battle my family or my Patriotism. I have my faith as many among us have. This government is laden with vial and demining motives. They seek more government while true patriots seek less government.

It is hard to understand from those ill in formed. Those on government handouts, Medicaid, Medicare, food stamps. Are you happy while the rest of us are paying for what you enjoy! The low life hypocrites are on a feeding frenzy and the AARP is right there on top. They are feeding on us like leaches, sucking the life blood out of our country, our Republic, our Liberty and our wallets. It is time to close the wallet, shut down all the Liberal programs, and put all families and individuals responsible for their own actions.

I say this with much distress and anxiety for I know how important it is to the progressive/liberal movement but they must wake up and understand this country can't continue down this path. If we do, it will drag everyone down the same path and what will we have then?

Before one goes on the people's (government) dowel, each needs to realize at some point the dowel will run out and then what? Then what will be the choices?

I fear we have driven ourselves into the abyss for total destruction

and if it continues this country will be lost for generations if not forever.

Everyone looks at government with big pockets and lots of cash to throw around but that is not the case and never will be. Our government creates programs to epées the people on Medicare, Medicaid with no monetary funds to sustain it, so they create more taxes from the working class, the ones that have a job and actually work 40 or more hours a week. How much more of their/our money do you want?

This is not a game we play with. This is real life!

Understanding real life is sometimes difficult but at some point, one has to face their choices in life. Not one taxpaying citizen made that choice for you, yet you want them to help you. There is something very wrong with this mind set and you know it, you just do not want the face it. So, get off your ass, find a job, and contribute to what you want. Then and only then will you understand what the rest of the working Americans are doing for you.

If you are a Christian and a Patriot you know what I am talking about, but if you are on the dowel then you may be somewhat puzzled?

Christians and Patriots under the current administration understand what is at stake and that is why they are the targets of the Liberals, Progressives, and Communists.

If you feel your passion in any of the three, then your soul will be with the rest of us while we are all standing in the same food isle, together, waiting for a meal while an illegal Alien, gang member, or a radical Muslim sets off a bomb and ends your wait in the food isle.

THEN IT REALLY DOES NOT MATTER ANYMORE!

CHOICES ARE AT HAND

Falling like Dominos

In the year 2012

Commentary: 01/05/2011

Be prepared for more changes from the Obama administration. His motives of circumventing the Constitution and the Bill of Rights are happening on a regular basis. He is determined to change this country to what he wants and desires regardless of how this country was founded.

My friends our rights are being dissolved everyday by this president and his actions. Just today he decided to make a recess appointment when congress was not at recess. That is un-Constitutional at best and congress should get off their lazy asses and over-ride his appointment. Should they choose not to do so, then they should be held accountable by the people and the people should oust all of them including this president.

The Obama administration in his efforts to retain his presidency established a hotline for illegal aliens at the taxpayers' expense to gain their vote in the 2012 elections. This man is corrupt and so is his total administration. They all reek of Chicago style politics and corruption and we all know how and what has happened in that city. It is terrible and crumbling before the people's very eyes, yet the people sit back and let it happen.

This administration has been fighting Arizona and 27 other states regarding illegal persons on American soil and treating them as though they have rights. They have no rights in the country for they are all law breakers and should be treated as such. Deport them and secure the borders even if it means manning the borders with 50,000 troops. Damn, how hard is it!

This administration looks at the American people like a deer looks in the head lights. Can't see them, hear them, nor care about them. He is focused on the un- constitutional motives he is putting into place.

The domino effect is coming for all Americans.

The American people need to look at what is coming at them from the other direction. We have the patriot conservatives going in one direction while the other 48% are looking at government. You know liberals, communists, and progressives.

If the American people could see and visualize what is ahead they might see something they have over-looked. There are always signs on this path of Freedom and Liberty if only we could see them.

For example: If you are a trucker, you observe what the trucks look like coming from the other direction. Much like grandma's weather forecasting, if the truck is wet, it's raining up the road; covered in snow and ice, there's frozen precipitation not too far away. Then there's looking at the sky on the horizon, the old mariner's "red sky in morning, sailor take warning" is excellent advice for truckers. The types of clouds or heavy dust in the air all indicate what's to come.

The dominos are falling, one by one and with them our rights, hopes and dreams.

Why can't the people see it? The people need to look at what government does, how they do it, and what impact it will have on their lives and their families for years to come. Be diligent and observe without bias. See it for what it is, not what it gives. Government can be your friend but be cautious what it does. Treat government like truckers treat on coming trucks, with caution.

George Washington stated many years ago his concerns with government. He said these words: "Government is not reason; it is not eloquence; it is force! Like Fire, it is a dangerous servant and fearful master."

Those words should have great meaning today for his words should be echoed across this land for what this Congress and the Obama administration are doing to our rights, our Constitution, our way of life and our futures!

Samuel Adams, 1776 stated: "If ever a time should come, when vain and aspiring men shall possess the highest seats in Government, our country will stand in need of its experienced patriots to prevent its ruin."

If the people look the other way instead of looking ahead and disregard what is coming,

THEN IT REALLY DOES NOT MATTER ANYMORE!

CHOICES ARE AT HAND

THE PUZZLE

In the year 2012

Commentary: 01/12/2012

The Puzzle is something that most men and women have yet to put together or understand. It lies on the board of its founding. It has many pieces and options but it will all always leak back to its pieces, regardless of the breakup of its sections and parts.

Breaking down the family, tearing apart the Country, will not fill the texts of the history books nor put the puzzle were it is placed. Each will have a place on the table and each will have a puzzle piece to put in the Puzzle.

Some pieces will seek control and mandates while others will have something far greater. Those that hold the pieces, not regulated by control of federal government, will seek something far more direct. Their place, May it be humble, will have a far greater voice on the table. Each will have a piece of the puzzle to place in the hearts of mankind.

The actions determined by Liberals, Communists, Democrats, and a host of others scattered across this globe that think they know but do not have a clue.

They will be met head on by those that know!

"A man can fail many times, but he isn't a failure until he begins to blame someone else."
 John Burroughs

Obama is in campaign mode and he is blaming everyone but himself for the problems he has created along with this congress.

"There is more in us than we know. If we can be made to see it, perhaps, for the rest of our lives, we will be unwilling to settle for less. "
  Kurt Hahn

This statement has resonated across this land from the T.E.A. Patriots; they are not willing to settle for less but expect and to expand on the bounty and opportunities given by the purpose of this country.

"Even if it's a little thing, do something for those who need help, something for which you get no pay but the privilege of doing it."
  Albert Schweitzer

Most, if not all Patriots give to those that have not, but when a government continues to take what is not there's it leaves less to give to those in need.

"We have not a cold war but a hot war for Liberty and Less government."
  Terry W. Bettis

Any time a government determines those in power know better and create more jobs in the public sector to monitor those in the private sector, then the red flags of our Republic are threatened.

This is what Obama's claim to fame is regarding job creation.

Growing government will only take more from those currently working.

"The more the plan fails the more the planners plan!" Terry W. Bettis

Obama's plan is falling like dominoes on the table. Congress is out there somewhere trying to pick up the pieces. In the mean time all the planners in the background are and will create something to turn the focus on a different plan. The planners will always be there to create a new plan to take this country down the path of social, Communistic control. They are bees in the hive.

"Politics has no place in Liberty, and Democracy has no place in a Republic." - Terry W. Bettis

Obama and company, his czars, this congress since 2007, have not a place in our Liberty. They are pre-determined to destroy our Liberty and our REPUBLIC. That will not stand for real men and women who believe in the REPUBLIC.

The United States is not a democracy as the main stream media might portray it. These states where created as a REPUBLIC. It is the one thing the progressives, liberals, and Communists can't get a hold of. The over-takers have struggled to circumvent it but the founders knew this.

The Founders embedded something that most of us/them have yet to see when they created the documents which Liberals, Democrats, and Communist will never understand and most T.E.A.

Patriots already know.

It is not I that will forgive and relinquish the empowering tribute; it will be up to the people to discover it.

We can't put like positives or negatives together for they reject one

another. If you have studied science, you will know what science is and what fiction is.

The Question?

Is it time for all of us to look at the reflection in the mirror?

"It is not up to us to determine the outcome of one's life. That question which is best left to our God. We should always fight for one's life and let God handle the rest in the end?"

"So, therefore, we will put up a peaceful fight, and if that doesn't work to save our lives, then we must resort to more drastic measures... Albeit against our will which prefers peace. "Give me liberty or give me death!" - Patrick Henry.

"If we sit around and wait too long, the war of ideas will be over before it has ever begun. We will lose. This cannot be allowed to happen much longer". - Jill Clayton

"God is still on the Throne, and still hears and answers prayers. We must never forget He is still the King of the universe, whether the arrogant powers on earth like it or not! "Alyssa Sue H.

There are many questions to this PUZZLE. It will be determined by the efforts of the people to put the pieces together. But in our haste, are we lacking in our focus? Will the puzzle go on UN-finished? Therefore, leaving a people in disarray and blurred in their vision of its meaning and bewildered in its outcome will only put more confusion in the minds of the Patriots and GOD fearing peoples.

Putting the pieces of the puzzle together is like putting your life together before you have lived it! Predetermined aspirations are in the law of GOD's hands and not in political leaders or takers.

We can't plan our life based on something that we have not lived or how we would like it to be. That would be like a puzzle already put together at the end of our life, move it around, break it apart and put the pieces back the way we want them.

If we could put the pieces together as we see them to determine the outcome of our lives, would it make us feel better? That is exactly what the Liberals desire, along with the Communists, Socialist, and Democrats.

Their motives are driven by destroying the family unit!!!! See it, Believe it, and Understand IT!!

This, my friends are not what GOD's intention were all about.

GOD,

"He did not give you death before life so you could rearrange life before death. He gave your life so you could enjoy the fruits of his

grace and mercy and be challenged during your life to always seek his wisdom during life and return to him for forgiveness should one stray."

Richard Stockton (1730-1781), a signer of the Declaration of Independence, was a member of the Continental Congress, 1776...In his will, Richard Stockton wrote:

"As my children will have frequent occasion of perusing this instrument and may probably be peculiarly impressed with the last words of their father, I think proper here, not only to subscribe to the entire belief of the great leading doctrine of the Christian religion...but also in the heart of a father's affection, to charge and exhort them to remember "that the fear of the Lord is the beginning of wisdom."

The future of our families, our children and our Liberty are at stake.

The path we choose will determine our future and the future of our Republic. Be wise in your choices and pray to GOD they will be the right choice.

CHOICES ARE AT HAND

What Happened Four Years Ago

Is the American People Really Looking forward to four more Years?
In the year 2012

Commentary: 02/05/2012

After the rant and back and forth of the democrats between Hilary and Obama, the opposition was left with a moderate Republican Liberal to run against the winner of the Democrat progressive. When the tally between the two final candidates was finally revealed, the people were left with two progressive choices. One on the left and one on the left but none would adhere to the Constitution or the Bill of Rights and the people were left with OBAMA. So here we are.

His record as of to date:

46% of the American people pay not one dime in taxes and often get a tax refund. While the other 54% pay the rest.

Obama admitted that some of the so called shovel ready jobs were not ready, yet he shut down the Canadian pipeline to Houston which would have created thousands of jobs.

Obama Care and its mandates are un-constitutional and the so called Supreme Court will be ruling if it be un-constitutional. The vote in the court should be by all means be an up or down vote, 9 for 9 for, or 9 for 9 against. There is no grey water to tread according the Constitution. If the vote is otherwise then neither is reading nor understanding what their oath is all incubuses in the rights and mandates in the Constitution.

All the money that this congress has let pass into the hands of Obama, his czars, and special interest groups should by all means be returned back to the people by those that have taken a path beyond the oath they took. Their oath did not say, "I will take from those that have and give to those that have not."

Obama took over two car companies, shut down off-shore drilling, and tore the heart out of a major industry which affected countless lives and business that depended on offshore drilling. Obama supported an electrical car made by GM, solar energy company that received billions in government money, (Tax Payers wealth) are going down faster than the Titanic. All are filing or will file for bankruptcy.

Obama has joined forces with foreign countries to sue a state that he swore an oath to protect which means his oath has not meaning in his agenda.

He took office with a 9 trillion dollar deficit; today that deficit is nearing the 16 trillion dollar milestone in just 3 ½ years. How much more will the people be subjected to before they have had enough?

This lazy ass Congress can't see the picture or they are not willing to turn the spikit off and turn this country around. The people are

in control of the money, not this congress, not this PRESIDENT, his czars, special interest groups, nor anyone but the people!

If congress will not do their jobs, they need to be replaced in the upcoming election with new flesh and vigor, ALL OF THEM. Old politics and playing the game on the hill has no place in our Republic. The people need to flush this sewer in Washington D. C. and put some real blood in the veins of the Republic.

Not a democracy, not special interest groups, not congress, not a president nor a judicial system. All have been corrupted by the system which they created. The only ones left holding the bag will be the people and to be quite honest the bag is too heavy for us to carry, and the people should refuse such a burdened.

It is times to drain the bag and put those that created this destructive mandate back on their plate and tell them to fix it or pay for it with their own money and not ours.

When will the Representatives (of the people) who walk into the halls of congress, owned by the people, paid by the people, and for the people, open our house and say: "The people have spoken and they want us to return home today but they have demanded that before this session is ended, on this day, we must cut 9 trillion in spending effective immediately, not ten years from today, but today!

One stipulation in their demands was to make sure it is within the bounds of the Constitution and the Bill of Rights. So ladies and gentlemen we have a lot of work to do, so let's get it done. I know

this will be hard for most if not all but you need to drag out that old dusty and tarnished document that created this country the (Constitution and the Bill of Rights), and start reading it, because at the end of this day we are going to do what the people have demanded.

The people are now in control and we were elected to serve the people. Our self interest, special interests and political ambitions must be put aside. The people have been asking us for years: "What has happened to the people and this Republic!" It is time we did the right thing for God, our Republic, and its PEOPLE.

Some of us and especially all those in Congress have fallen into the trap of progressive motives and ambitions of outright control by the Liberal, Progressive motives. We have yielded to our enemy when we should be facing the enemy head on. So let us all get this done.

It is time for T.E.A. Patriots to stand once again, to make our voices heard; it is time for the takeover of this Liberal, Progressive government

"All it takes for evil to triumph is for good men and women to do nothing."

Obama and company and this Congress can push the people so far before something breaks. I feel we are reaching the breaking point!

Is there one or many out there willing to stand with us for what is right according to the Constitution and Bills of Rights?

CHOICES ARE AT HAND

Oligarchic Dictatorship

Is the American People Really Looking forward to OUR Future?
In the year 2012

Commentary: 02/10/2012

Before you read this be aware of your Republic and what is means, even if you have not chosen to find out what a REPUBILC is?

On January 4th, 2012, I wrote an article: "If you are Christian and a Patriot" you are the target of this administration and all that follow him. In that article I wrote this:

"If you are a Christian and a Patriot then you have become the targets of the radical Muslims, illegal aliens, War lords, Gangs from all backgrounds led by the drug wars and their motives and <u>most important a government that has excepted an Oligarchic Dictatorship, for control.</u> In their attempt to take control, the one thing in the equation left out, was a Christian and a Patriot.

The Liberals, Progressives, Communists, Wall Street marchers, and Radicals running rampant in this land have left behind, for just cause, the Christian and Patriots. That will be their misgiving of their own demise."

Obama is giving handouts to all that seek to follow him in favor of votes with this mandate of a social program that stomps on the fundamental rights of the first Amendment, tramples on our RELIGIOUS freedoms and RIGHTS.

Mandates from a President without due process from CONGRESS or course in the Constitutional founding of this land can't stand. The people know this! It appears that this President OBAMA and company are determined to fundamentally change this REPUBLIC into a SOCIAL sphere of an unknown ABYSS.

He favors the destruction of this REPUBLIC in order to gain control of the Peoples Rights under an abyss of deceptions of women's rights based on a political move to gain favor with women, just for their vote. This act to tear down the Religious Freedoms of a People, steps outside the bounds of his authority and tramples on the free speech in this country for all, not just those that can see this mutilation of rights, but for all that can't see it today but will feel it in times future, be it from the left or right but for all people.

Congress sites on their behinds while the president (OBAMA) continues to shred the founding documents that should hold him in check and protect the PEOPLE.

When Congress passed the mandated bill, we call: Obama Care, it opened a wide area of options and mandates that the president by law can mandate. This congress has fallen victim of their own votes and as such has violated their oaths and have put the people in the sewer they have created for us all. It is time for those in congress to stand in the same sewer they have put us in!"WILL THEY STAND WITH THE PEOPLE AND DO SOMETHING TO CORRECT THE PROBEMS THEY CREATED! If fear not, for they have fell into the trap.

POWER BEGETS POWER!

We all stand on a preface, be it low income, middle income or upper income. All were given the same openings in life to create and do as one desires. Sometimes the outcomes we took were not desirable for our future. Life is not granted in iron blocks or by granite stone. Life is soft and pure and with meaning without outside influences.

We all know those that have managed to crawl out of the deception, the rules and regulations, and the unknown abyss of what is waiting in the overall structure of this REPUBLIC, have done so by sure motivation in their efforts.

There was a book written: "The Theory and practice of OLIGARCHIAL Collectivism." by Emmanuel Goldstein

(The Book within a Book' from George Orwell's Nineteen Eighty-Four

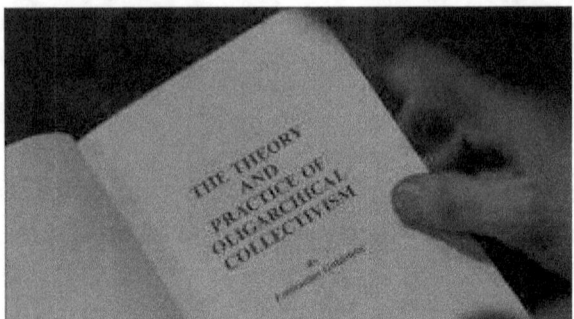

In the book it is stated in Chapter I:

Ignorance is Strength:

"Throughout recorded time, and probably since the end of the Neolithic Age, there have been three kinds of people in the world, the High, the Middle, and the Low.

They have been subdivided in many ways, they have borne countless different names, and their relative numbers, as well as their attitude towards one another, have varied from age to age: but the essential structure of society has never altered. Even after enormous upheavals and seemingly irrevocable changes, the same pattern has always reasserted itself, just as a gyroscope will always return to equilibrium, however far it is pushed one way or the other.

The aims of these three groups are entirely irreconcilable. The aim of the High is to remain where they are. The aim of the Middle is to change places with the High. The aim of the Low, when they have an aim   for it is an abiding characteristic of the Low that they are too much crushed by drudgery to be more than intermittently conscious of anything outside their daily lives   is to abolish all distinctions and create a society in which all men shall be equal. Thus, throughout history a struggle which is the same in its main outlines recurs over and over again. For long periods the High seem to be securely in power, but sooner or later there always comes a moment when they lose either their belief in themselves or their capacity to govern efficiently, or both. They are then overthrown by the Middle, who enlist the Low on their side by pretending to them that they are fighting for liberty and justice. As soon as they have reached their objective, the Middle thrust the Low back into their old position of servitude, and themselves become the High. Presently a new Middle group splits off from one of the other groups, or from both of them, and the struggle begins over again. Of the three groups, only the Low are never even temporarily successful in achieving their aims. It would be an exaggeration to say that throughout history there has been no progress of a material kind. Even today, in a period of decline, the average human being is physically better off than he was a few centuries ago. But no advance in wealth, no softening of manners, no reform or revolution has ever brought human equality a millimeter nearer. From the point of view of the Low, no historic change has ever meant much more than a change in the name of their masters..."

http://www.youtube.com/watch?NR=1&feature=endscreen&v=spl-C882yiM

One must read between the lines of the video and understand that there are evil intentions among us.

Chapter II

Freedom is Slavery
(Ommited from book)

Chapter III

War is Peace

The splitting up of the world into three great super-states was an event which could be and indeed was foreseen before the middle of the twentieth century. With the absorption of Europe by Russia and of the British Empire by the United States, two of the three existing powers, Eurasia and Oceania, were already effectively in being. The third, East Asia, only emerged as a distinct unit after another decade of confused fighting. The frontiers between the three super-states are in some places arbitrary, and in others they fluctuate according to the fortunes of war, but in general they follow geographical lines. Eurasia comprises the whole of the northern part of the European and Asiatic land-mass, from Portugal to the Bering Strait. Oceania comprises the Americas, the Atlantic islands including the British Isles, Australasia, and the southern portion of Africa. East Asia, smaller than the others and with a less definite western frontier, comprises China and the countries to the south of it, the Japanese islands and a large but fluctuating portion of Manchuria, Mongolia, and Tibet.

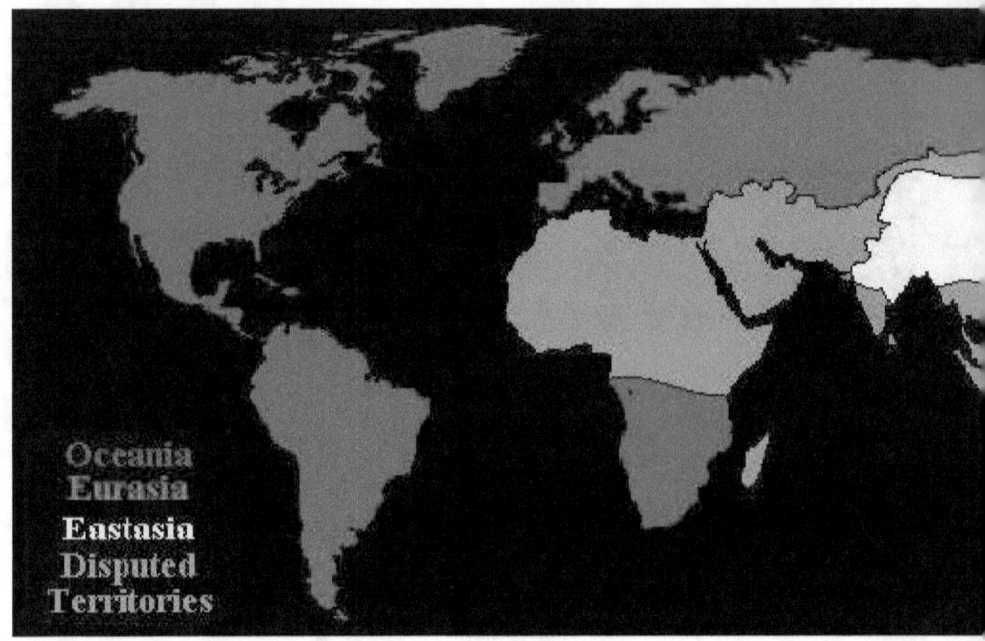

Oceania
Eurasia
Eastasia
Disputed
Territories

http://www.newspeakdictionary.com/go-goldstein.html

"In each variant of Socialism that appeared from about 1900 onwards the aim of establishing liberty and equality was more and more openly abandoned. The new movements which appeared in the middle years of the century . . . had the conscious aim of perpetuating un-freedom and inequality"; because the true goal was to end history upon becoming the perpetual High ruling class   composed not of aristocrats or plutocrats, but of "bureaucrats, scientists, technicians, trade- union organizers, publicity experts, sociologists, teachers, journalists and professional politicians" originally from "the salaried middle class and the upper grades of the working class".

http://www.redstate.com/repair_man_jack/2011/04/05/it%E2%80%99s-oligarchical-collectivism-or- shutdown/

"Inequality is back in the news, largely thanks to Occupy Wall Street, but with an assist from the Congressional Budget Office. And you know what that means: It's time to roll out the obfuscators!

Anyone who has tracked this issue over time knows what I mean. Whenever growing income disparities threaten to come into focus, a reliable set of defenders tries to bring back the blur. Think tanks put out reports claiming that inequality isn't really rising, or that it doesn't matter. Pundits try to put a more benign face on the phenomenon, claiming that it's not really the wealthy few versus the rest, it's the educated versus the less educated.

So what you need to know is that all of these claims are basically attempts to obscure the stark reality: We have a society in which money is increasingly concentrated in the hands of a few people, and in which that concentration of income and wealth threatens to make us a democracy in name only…

http://www.nytimes.com/2011/11/04/opinion/oligarchy-american-style.html

As one has read in the above comments and referenced the links where do the American people fit in the overall picture of this nation's future? I personally think that as long as the people and the political leaders continue to think America is a democracy and not a republic they will continue to divide and conquer. In that concept we must put GOD back in this venue for that venue is where it all began.

It is time for T.E.A. Patriots to stand once again, to make our voices heard; is it time for the takeover of this Liberal, Progressive government and put it on notice?

"All it takes for evil to triumph is for good men and women to do nothing."

Obama and company and this Congress can push the people so far before something breaks. I feel we are reaching the breaking point!

Is there one or many out there willing to stand with us for what is right according to the Constitution and Bills of Rights?

CHOICES ARE AT HAND

The War of Minds

It has been spoken that the United States has fought the longest war in our history in Afghanistan. Ten years in the making but is there another?

In the year 2012

Commentary: 02/14/2012

We as a people often think of WAR as men with weapons, armaments and such as are needed in WAR. The killing field on the actual battle leaves torn bodies and death and destruction of human life, souls, families and property misplaced and broken. Both sides loose in the total picture of the war and the battles which were fought will remain.

What is left out of the equation is the War in the Minds of the PEOPLE! Is it based on a religious foundation, a moral foundation, or a lack of understanding? Questions for all to think about as our Republic and Rights are melting in the lava of the Roman Empire?

We stand this day in the year 2012 with many questions regarding the future of this Republic we dwell in. There is a battle among the people since 1893 what government's role plays in the lives, and futures of a people. It has raged for decades, crossed the paths of many Presidents desk and Congressional leaders. Each took a step in their moment of history to try and fix-it. But in their efforts only created a bigger obligation and burden upon the very ones they were trying to assist.

First of all, a government can't fix anything and it is not obligated to do such. A government is put in place to protect the rights of all people without due course, in self, but stand on the bands of the will of the people and be just in their efforts. The people desire not handouts from a government, for the government was created by the people that elected them.

When the people see government as a striking force against them, WHEN all the people desired was Liberty, property, and opportunity.

Not restrictions, rules, mandates, laws of unjust congressional leaders, but total freedom from all such acts as lay upon the people we are currently living. What has transpired over the decades has put much burden in the hearts and minds of its citizens and has laid a great divide among the people. Is this what a Republic was designed?

We have all seen the wars of minds over the decades; the battles are still fought even into day's media. Sides drive the force between the motivations and put the people in the middle to make choices. Deciding between two evil forces leaves only evil in the division.

So, all we have to look at is the War of the Minds, when all we had to do is look and hold dear in our hearts and spirit, what the Founders gave us.

"All it takes for evil to triumph is for good men and women to do nothing."

Is there one or many out there willing to stand with us for what is right according to the Constitution and Bills of Rights?

CHOICES ARE AT HAND

Our First Right and Last Right

Is the American People Really Looking forward to OUR Future?
In the year 2012

Commentary: 02/13/2012

Those of you who have personal beliefs that your Christianity requires passive submission with no resistance to evil, then understand that your belief system is the same type that the German and Russian Christians had that gave birth to Hitler and Stalin. All it takes for evil to prevail is for good people to do nothing.

To remain silent in the face of radical corruption makes cowards of men and leads to the mass murder of millions.

What this administration (Obama) is forcing on the 1st Amendments rights of all Americans with a mandate on religious rights, disguised as women's rights for medical assurance, is pure nonsense.

The people must look through the fog and see the real picture.

Should this administration get away with the destruction of our 1st Right under the Bill of Rights then he will move forward to the 2nd right and paint it with a broad brush with some tauter that will among a few seem OK, and before we know it, we will have lost all our rights and the ability to defend the rights we once had.

There is a big difference between lawful authority and a criminal usurper like Obama. The problem is that many of us are too ignorant to know the difference!

Focus on the issue at hand. Mandates from any government is a recurrence and pre-cursors of any Marxists, Communist, Social, Progressive agenda that begins the process of total and outright control of its people, lifestyles and Freedoms.

On many occasions throughout the Bible, God's people used armed force to overthrow tyranny. Scriptures clearly show that God never viewed a tyrannical power as a legitimate government. Just because an elite group was in power because of their weapons, they were not viewed as the government ordained of God, because God never ordains tyranny. Thus, God never commands His people to view tyranny as a valid authority.

Tearing down the freedoms and rights of people for a government to gain more control, be it religious or otherwise will always be outside the realm of its power in a Republic.

But since most Americans think we live in a democracy it will be hard to turn them toward the Republic they used to currently enjoy.

It is apparent that this REPUBLIC is under attack and the forces leading it are but subtle minds as young children.

"We have hostile forces among us to the tune of millions of Obama Youth, illegal drug gangs from Mexico who are former military themselves, foreign troops on American military bases, militant homosexuals that would just as soon kill you as look at you and of course finally, millions of Muslims just waiting in the wings to commence their orchestrated attacks on the American people. Unfortunately, the most pressing issue for many Americans is who is going to win the super bowl last weekend and oh yes, American Idol has begun again for a new season. Our clueless generation is about to pay a heavy price for their total ignorance!"

GOD help us and bless us, for the people are blinded in the fog of destruction and control by a civil politic without you.

Is there one or many out there willing to stand with us for what is right according to the Constitution and Bills of Rights?

CHOICES ARE AT HAND

"All it takes for evil to triumph is for good men and women to do nothing."

Obama and company and this Congress can push the people so far before something breaks. I feel we are reaching the breaking point!

Is there one or many out there willing to stand with us for what is right according to the Constitution and Bills of Rights?

CHOICES ARE AT HAND

The Moral Compass of the Leaders

Is the American People Really Looking forward to FOUR more Years?

In the year 2012

Commentary: 03/06/2012

There lies no moral compass, when the leader of a free Republic, our President OBAMA, of the United States, will take his valuable time to speak to a Scarlet Letter branded individual over a menial, **staged** broadcast to benefit his corrupt and despicable intensions'. We stand on this day with a country that is divided in its parts and even more by its emotions. This president and congress have created a COMPASS of unknown outcome and the arrows have no direction.

In concept, we are facing a moral break down in our heritage, culture warriors, and religious beliefs.

We have a president filing laws suites against states and their rights such as Arizona which in the total of summation allows illegals to gain benefit from this Republic.

I find this puzzling, when his moral compass should be looking at the people with all of its parts not a selected few gremlin rolling around the land, devouring everything in its path for self gratification and fulfillment, while the other 50% pays for it?

This picture painted is disturbing at most but should be a shocker to all!

There lies no Honor in this administration. Its mission seems to be motivated by self destruction in all of it parts of this Republic.

This administration seeks only control in the whole but leaves out the concept of moral compass against its people and why not! That is how the compass has turned to their political venue of the so-called leaders of a non-informed politic.

There is no North or South, East, or West in the compass of his motives, poised by this president with his minions, czars and activists, standing in wait to attack the very heart and soul of our Republic.

It all starts from the top down which is what they seek. The so-called leaders of a free nation feel betrayed because they have yet to get all they seek.

This Republic never started from the top down. It started from the bottom up and the concept will never be in the mindset of progressive/liberals as they continue to find ways to reverse the process.

We have a president that has no moral compass regarding the Republic. He refers to this country as a Democracy.

We have a congress that has no moral compass regarding the Republic, for they too agree with this president that this country is a Democracy.

We as a people are standing on the edge of a total social, Marxist takeover of our Republic. Even Obama and company have stated that he needs 5 more years to complete his mission. Should the American people relinquish and give him this

election in November 2012, to complete his mission, then we will be subjected to a deficit that will rise beyond unknown expandability and the compass will be turned into a whirl wind of undesired outcome.

At that point the teeth and bite of their motives will move in and consume this Republic and we will be subjected to an extreme, overpowering government with more regulations and control of our lives.

When Obama, the President, came into office the deficit was 9 trillion, today it's over 16 trillion. He and this Congress have created this is less than four years of his presidency. There should be an alarm going off in every man, women, and child's pocketbook! If we can't see this future picture, then we deserve what we can't see!

Big government is their motive! This government is consuming our Republic and our Liberty. This administration, and many before him, has motives, along with the liberals and the Alinsky plan, are driving forward their intentions to control every aspect of the American politic.

Their total motives have been seen for years passed when a baby

was born, not aborted, to get a social security card to prove they were born. What a piece of work by this government, and the people did not even see it coming. That was then but this in now.

The entire Compass of the left be they democrats, liberals, socialist, or outright communists, is to take down our way of life and control us from the birthing room to the grave. But if they can get you before the birthing room and use their groups of anti-people and pro-government, using the likes as the ACLU, the SPLC, the ADL, Planned Parenthood and the many other organizations created by communists and leftist to take down our way of life, there will be no life. That little life will be counted as another one to add to the over 50 million babies that have been aborted since Roe v Wade.

They, the Liberal, Progressive, and Communists have been privileged to accomplish this vial treatment of humankind, but rejoice in their motives and accomplishments which have taken down our moral compass as CHRISTIANS and our way of LIFE and most important how this country was founded.

It is time for true AMERICANS that believe in a REPUBLIC to stand true. The destruction of the moral fiber of a people is indoctrinated by the Progressive movement to tear down our moral and Christian way of life in the fiber of their compass to destroy this Republic and its people.

Their concept is imbedded in their IMMORALL fiber by indoctrination, of the social ill-informed, and in doing so using the Militant feminism, militant gay activists, militant atheists…

(ACLU), to gain favor in their mission.

It is high time we stand up and fight for CHRIST and our REPUBLIC! IT is time to tell the left "Enough is Enough"!

It is time we stand as one and fight for CHRIST and our REPUBLIC, one vote at a time, one community at a time, one CHURCH at a time!

Well, (as Ronald Reagan said often in many speeches and debates) that one word. WELL, with a little smile on his face.

WELL?

CHOICES ARE AT HAND

Vestige

Is the American People Really Looking forward to FOUR more Years?
In the year 2012

Commentary: 03/20/2012

Tonight's words of wisdom: "As our house is slowly deteriorating in an unjust atmosphere of political evil, driven by non-constitutional means, we must look beyond their motives and take the necessary preparations to secure one's family and maybe a little extra for family and friends set aside that may not have the means.

Fuel costs and heating oil will continue to rise in the coming months so stock up if you can. As Obama has stated on many occasions in his many speeches over the years, He desires higher fuel costs.

Get a plan together for food stock, water and power, at least enough to last for four years if Obama and company if they remain in power after the 2012 election."

If you can, buy propane, it will last forever. Put in a propane generator but have plenty of oil to feed it if you run it 24-7 and a 1000-gal tank. It is clean burning, cheap compared to days cost of other fuels. Stock up on firewood and liters.

Lantern fuel, matches, tents, sleeping bags and most it not the most important, Weapons. You know, guns, shot guns, deer rifles and others if you can afford. Make sure you have plenty of ammo to for each and teach all in the household how to use them safely.

Fighting tyranny on our own soil of this Republic, from our elected officials is puzzling at least but it has grasped the jugular of our being and the heart and soul of this Republic.

The Republic was lost years ago when a democratic form of Progressives and power hungry vultures came into power. Obama is not the first, but with God's help and true believing PATRIOTS, he will be the last!

The serpent (Obama and Company) has wrapped its forked tongue around the whole of this nation. The venom is soaking our Rights, our Republic and our Liberty in a poisonous ejaculation of self gratification secreted by manmade motives and destruction's.

All this administration has done the last three and a half years has vex the people. This vexation has only caused a vexatious feeling in this country and for all the people there in.

So why, would I tell all to prepare?

The versant must understand what is happening!

CHOICES ARE AT HAND

What is a Socialist

Is the American People Really Looking forward to FOUR more Years?
In the year 2012

Commentary: 03/23/2012

Tonight's words of wisdom: "What is a Socialist"? We have all read this word in blogs, on FB, Freedom Torch, twitter and a multitude of web sites, news outlets, from prime time to cable, but what does this one word really mean? Is this one word the preamble to a far greater motive in its concept?

Such as: Socialism, Social service, social science, social security, social studies, social-minded, social insurance, social work and a monumental barrage of other terms and meanings? We can reference this word and all the other social attached words in other meanings that have created this atmosphere, but would one understand? It was created by a motive that has relished across the dictionaries, textbooks and teachings in our schools and planted in the mindset of the people for over a century.

The sad part, we did nothing then and know we are doing nothing today, at this point in our history, so why are we complaining?

The concept in its meaning drew me back to a time when these words were not even in the vocabulary of men and women thoughts. It was not in print; it was not growing in the people's hearts or its leaders from the Federal level to the state and local level. It did not exist. So, what happened? That my friends will be the fundamental question we must ask ourselves!

The word Socialist has been thrown around this country for so long that none understands Its true meaning and care not to find out. It will be the un-excepted practice of a far greater enemy that most have yet to come face-to-face-with. But we all will!

Once the gears are set (by the Socialists) in place and the aroma of victory can be smelled from the start of the beginning of destruction, it will be too late for the people. Once the engine that drives those gears is ribbed up to its objective then, what? Should that time come…?

We as a people can search all the dictionaries currently in writing and read about the social issues and message which have been cemented in the minds of the so-called wisdom of the definitions in their writings but have had an over empowering outcome in our thoughts and motives. The definitions have been left out of the words or word which were never taught in the public (government) schools and for most were never there.

I understand that most will not understand what I just wrote, but the facts are written in the words as defined. Finding the true meaning may be hard for some and others will cover it over with political mindsets still playing on the playground of the mindless 1% that seem to think their motives will gain them something far greater in the overall spectrum, while others will seeks the wisdom which created them.

So, let's have a thought:

When we focus on current events without knowledge or a desire to seek it then what? In the book of Proverbs, chapter 29:2 "When the righteous are in authority,

the people rejoice: but when the wicked beareth rule, the people morn." So where are we today?

The control of a people, its states, will never stand among men, rules, regulations, or mandates; it will always be driven by the people! The people will never be willing to give up what is theirs. Why are we giving up?

The American people have never given-up or are willing to give into a government that desires to control them. So, my friends, let's take a look at the words or word.

After The Declaration of Independence was declared by the people of the Colonies from the British King the word Socialist was not there. When the colonies won that victory and gained their independence from British rule, and by doing so, created the Constitution, Bill of Rights and with it three separate levels of government, unheard of in any history known to man and with it created the greatest country ever!

This evening, I attempted to search the word Socialist, but all the results came back to Socialism. This is my search: "first appearance of the word socialist."

We must understand the enemy before we can destroy it!

In the Noah Webster dictionary of 1828, the word Socialist or Socialism are not there, but when one searches the definitions of this word in a more current version of any dictionary, such as Webster's seventh New Collegiate Dictionary, the word Socialist is defined and related to many other words and definitions. All related back to the same objective.

My friends, we are fighting a battle of knowledge and understanding. The precepts being taught in the government schools and we continue the lead our children into this vial and corrupted venue of mist-education, should look at the motives. That is what it is!

A Socialist mist is blowing across this country and has been for generations. The motivation of a Socialist is to change the young into believing in a government to take care of them, without knowledge of the outcome. Should they follow and disregard the founding documents laid before us, as a people, blessed by our Christian, GOD, or will they be consumed by the Socialist mist?

After the Revolution in the 1776, even up to the time of 1828, those two words were never mentioned. So, what changed?

I pray this eve that the people will understand and seek the knowledge necessary to right the wrongs and seek the wisdom of our God and the wisdom of our Founders.

CHOICES ARE AT HAND

Loyalist versus Patriots

Is the American People Really Looking forward to FOUR more Years?
In the year 2012

Commentary: 04/01/2012

My heart breaths deep in my soul as our rights as citizens may take a turn towards the dark side of our Liberty and Freedoms and we as a people will be subjected to a government that has grown beyond is Constitutional authority and its GOD given rights and has crowned itself as the solution!

This is a question we must ask ourselves in this current time. Do we as a people expect to conquer in war or are we willing to be subjects?

If so, war is no longer simple, but when we as a people seek the realms of our founding will we be found in contempt of the Conqueror and its objectives?

Striking down a formable foe that was given opportunity in this Republic will be most difficult but not outside the reach of the Patriots or those which have been chosen to fix it.

In a comment on FB noted: by Lisa Koon Hernandez (with permission) in quotes, she said the following:
"Life was never promised to be easy and as I read all of my FB status updates from friends and family... I can tell those of us who have the good Lord in our lives from those of them who don't. Some of the post our filled with fear, violence, depression, ignorance, and so much negativity and then some of the post our filled with strength, peace, happiness, wisdom, and positivity... NO it's not because Christians lives are easier, or they are any better than anybody else

but it's because WE HAVE THE GOOD LORD WHO IS THERE WITH US TO CARRY US THROUGH! We know we cannot conquer this world on our own and HE is with us ALWAYS! We can do anything through Christ who strengthens us!!! WE ARE NOTHING WITHOUT HIM!"

One only must look outside the backdoor of their creation and meaning. We have been soaked up into a world of Liberal thinkers which in its whole can't change it if we have what we have. Why they are so determined to change it, in its parts by scrapping away at its foundation?

Loyalists seek total control of its power, be it within the three branches of our government of HOPE and CHANGE though subversion into the dark side of our LIBERTY and FREEDOMS or will the wisdom of the Patriots be the ultimate outcome?

Loyalist sees this as a venue of opportunity while Patriots see this as a battle hymn for this Republic.

Wisdom only comes from knowledge and the Loyalist's knew that and that is why in years past they planted a seed that has grown beyond its teaching. It grew as a pimple on our REPUBLIC and has created a BOIL on OUR LIBERTY.

It is festering in the skin of the REPUBLIC! Why are the schools the way they are? Why are the laws so subversive and leaning outside the documents of our Founders?

Loyalist has been given great power from the people and what they do has created division among the peoples. Seeing through their visions may be the outright control of everything or a waking call for the PATRIOTS!

I may stand checked but we as a people must become unchecked to right the wrongs. We must think outside the box of Loyalist and focus on the Republic in all of it parts, From the Declaration to the Constitution and the Bill of Rights in all of its parts and seek the wisdom of our GOD which created it!

Silent talk has much meaning, passing the message with great voice may also be unheard, but the Silent message and our future may lay in the Loyalists message, for their message is far greater and deeper in its motives.

Will the message be heard or understood by the Patriots and are they willing to take it on?

The Loyalist have always sent their message in silent talk and roads that lead to nowhere for the people but has been cemented on the path they are creating that paints a path of freedom and deception that will be soaked in a slime one will be crawling from for countless years, IF NOT GENERATIONS.

Loyalist has no place in a REPUBLIC but is most comforted in a Democracy!

THIS COUNTRY WAS NOT CREATED AS A DEMOCRACY; IT IS A REPUBLIC.

I pray this eve that the people will understand and seek the knowledge necessary to right the wrongs and seek the wisdom of our God and the wisdom of our Founders.

CHOICES ARE AT HAND

Where Will We be Tomorrow

Is the American People Really Looking forward to FOUR more Years?
In the year 2012

Commentary: 04/04/2012

Are we as a people ready and aware of what it will take to correct this mess we have let happen? Are we really prepared for tomorrow? Where will be tomorrow?

We had a Declaration, then we had a constitution, which in its means created three parts of the governing body, and then we had the Bill of Rights.

Is each part of its elements outside its Constitutional realm? If so, is our path as citizens of this great land, predetermined or is it being subverted in its meaning? In the prospective of our Founders, to those who sacrificed for our freedom, was the end worth the painful means? We as a people have shamelessly challenged our founding and have done the one thing that the founders would not adhere; we have given our government to evil men and women, with more power and control than any before us.

How would the founders of this great land, after great sacrifice, look upon us?

Should we be ashamed? What they did should be admired, what we have done with it should be questioned and shameful!

Today, we look at this government as the answer for all problems. We expect the all-powerful government to fix everything. Is this the path we as a people should be seeking?

I question it only because of what Thomas Paine, 1776, stated:" What we obtain too cheaply, we esteem too lightly; it is dearness only that gives everything its value. Heaven knows how to put a proper price upon its goods; and it would be strange indeed if so celestial an article as FREEDOM should not be highly rated."

What was given to us as Americans of these United States appears to have been taken in vain by the people and left in the hands of men and women that have twisted its motives of Freedom and Liberty into a stream of laws, mandates and obstruction that is know feeding on the people and their minds. We as a people MUST start to see through this misty fog and read between the lines. If we choose not, then we as a people will be like all other countries across this globe, victims of government control!

Obama and company are spraying this mist of deceit across this land all the while talking about backstage deals with the Russians and then questioning the three branches of government, especially his health care bill currently being decided by the Supreme Court. He is playing on a thin layer of ice, and he knows it. Just today he toned down his rhetoric, but the cat is all ready out of the bag.

I have noticed in his new back drops in his speeches the American flag has once again appeared, but for the last three and half years there has been only a yellow rug or curtain behind him. It is obvious that he is trying to change his power image and draw away from his so-called Hope and Change election motive of three years past. What does that mean? (Deception and cleaver tactics!)

Cleaver backdrops and props can't change what he is doing, what he has done or what he is about to do, it he is re-elected!

We the people must be very attentive to everything this man (Obama) does. He is very cleaver and subtle in his motives. Obama has no record to run own and that is why he will twist the facts in his favor and those willing to fix it will be seen as the enemy to all Americans, especially, who's that can't see through the mist.

In the last three years this man (*Obama* and Company, *Reid, Pelosi*) have not upheld their Constitutional oath and demands based on the Constitution. They have run this country for three years without a budget and are turning it into a welfare state were opportunity and success will only be determined by:

HIS STATE.

Then Thomas Paine said: "Government, even in its best state, is but a necessary evil; in its worst state, an intolerable one."

He also stated: *"The duty of a PATRIOT is to protect his country from its government."*

Those of us that can see what is happening will have a most difficult time translating it to those that are blinded by the mist of deceit and deception! That will be the biggest challenge before us, if we are to regain this Republic.

Before that time comes, one thing that Thomas Paine stated was this: "If there must be trouble, let it be in my day, that my child may have peace."

Think about the enormity of this for just a few seconds…

We as a PEOPLE have been terrorized by our political system, our politicians, and our liberal media plenty for decades. Some of them have been checked, removed and others are relishing in their so-called victories. The resonance of the American People is outstanding. Most have seen this coming for decades and others will soon see it. Do not feel bad for not knowing about the government's motives, because, they have tried to hide this from the American public for decades. That's an undeniable fact. All one must seek is wisdom and question everything, everything that commends, regaled with the slime out of political men and women mouths and the corporate controlled mainstream media.

The corporate mainstream media has failed us: "We the People." As Ronald Reagan would say, "Well?"

And as the "Entrepreneur's Credo" Tomas Pain in brief:

"I do not choose to be a common man, it is my right to be uncommon… if I can, I seek opportunity…not security. I do not wish to be a kept citizen. Humbled and dulled by having the state look after me. I want to take the calculated risk; to dream and to build, to fail and to succeed. I refuse to barter incentive for a dole. I prefer the challenges of LIFE…"

So, with all this in mind, what are our choices? Is it in our heritage to stand erect, Proud, and unafraid; to think and act for oneself to enjoy the benefits of this Republic or will be subjected to tyranny?

Choices are at hand!

Comments regarding the book

Terry,

As always being a Christian and a patriot you are spot on! The tsunami of the progressive has grown from a ground swell to a tidal wave in less than 75 years. The drug of choice to put America at ease and tell all of us "everything is okay" go back to what you were doing while I increase your taxes, put more citizens on welfare and indoctrinate your children to MY history and philosophy is powerful!

To say the least!

I really like your analogy of the Alamo and the Texians fight for Independence. My 5th cousin was Sam Houston... Need I say more? You can put it any way you like but the silent majority is awake and not really happy with being drugged and duped! In my little sphere of influence here, many people have awoken and are rising to meet the challenge. It feels like the Alamo! But like Col. Travis, we have drawn the line in the sand and those who truly believe in Freedom and the Republic will make a stand even at the cost of our lives should they be required!

We as Patriots and fellow Christians need to unite in that same determination as the 183 did at the Alamo. Patriots like you and me are doing all we can to wake America up from that drugged slumber the progressives and communists have duped us with. And as with my cousin Sam Houston, I will accept no less than the return of our freedom and our Republic!

God Bless and have a happy new and victorious year. Roger

I have had the honor of reading Terry Bettis' book, Turning Points. Beginning with important history and progressing through what has happened to our Republic over the years since its inception, helps one understand what we are seeing today (2012).

Turning Points, as the title suggests, good or bad, have affected this country, leaving us with the America we are looking at now. While the people of this country have been asleep at the wheel for many generations, we have lost far more then we have gained. We now face a dictatorship that is enslaving us all.

Read this book. Learn from the points in our history where we "The People" have been sold a bill of goods. We need to understand what has happened in order to turn things around and save this great country that God blessed us with. May God guide each reader to action and understanding?

Gail Odegaard
Wyoming

Where to find our Books

Terry W. Bettis and Billie K. Bettis have other books that can be found:

Look for the following titles:

Guards at the Gate: How to win the War at Home
The Spiral Notebook: How our Live Changed Forever www.bteam.net

Turning Points: How Deception Steals Freedoms.
www.authorreputationpress.com
Barnes and Noble
Amazon
Go only to those sites to get the real books. Anywhere else may be a pirated copy from some foreign country or entity.